SINGLE, WHOLE AND HOLY

Christian Women and Sexuality

Joy Jacobs
and
Deborah Strubel

HORIZON BOOKS
CAMP HILL, PENNSYLVANIA

Dedicated to Julie Fehr

HORIZON BOOKS
3825 Hartzdale Drive
Camp Hill, PA 17011
www.cpi-horizon.com
www.christianpublications.com

ISBN: 0-88965-125-6
© 1996 by Horizon Books
All rights reserved
Printed in the United States of America

00 01 02 03 04   7 6 5 4 3

Contents

SINGLE, WHOLE
AND HOLY

Foreword

In the introduction to *Single, Whole and Holy: Christian Women and Sexuality* authors Joy Jacobs and Deborah Strubel state that this compassionate book deals with "subjects that are difficult to verbalize, and inappropriate for male pastors or counselors to discuss in depth with women." I agree. And in reading it, I must confess as a male, I felt at times like I was overhearing an intimate conversation between an older woman and a younger one. The advice was not for my ears, yet was fascinating.

However, there were times when I wanted to turn around and interject the perspective of a Christian male journalist! Their invitation to write this foreword—an inexplicable honor—gives me that opportunity.

Both Mrs. Jacobs and Mrs. Strubel speak with acute memory of their years as single women, but with the seasoned perspective of having lived in a good marriage and counseled other women. Unlike most counselors, however, they allow themselves to be vulnerable—acknowledging their own difficulties in the battleground of sex and the single woman. That makes their call to sexual purity authentic, credible and particularly helpful to single women in the late 1990s.

It is important to note that the so-called "sexual revolution" is largely a female revolution. Males have always been more promiscuous than females. But there has not been a great increase in sexually active males. By contrast, most females historically have been inclined to be chaste, perhaps out of the fear of pregnancy. But with "the pill" and other forms of birth control, even young girls have become more sexually active. As recently as 1970, only 29 percent of girls aged 15 to 19 had engaged in premarital sex. By 1988, it was 51.5 percent. For 18-year-olds, it rose from 39 percent to 69 percent. Whereas females used to say no, they often now say yes.

There are often tragic consequences—not only millions contracting sexually transmitted diseases and 1.2 million out-of-wedlock births a year—but also the guilt. As Deborah Strubel openly acknowledges, "My furious search for love and my lack of sexual boundaries was ruining my life. . . . I didn't have the courage to say no when I needed to, or to break off the parasitic relationship."

Mrs. Strubel writes that when she sacrificed her "self-respect in order to gain his approval," it didn't work anyway. He abandoned her.

Therefore, in her next relationships she learned to depend "on God, not my boyfriend, to meet my needs." That is an important lesson single women need to learn. And it can be learned in advance!

The Christian woman faces the potential of hell on earth if she abandons God's call to "flee from sexual immorality," as St. Paul put it in First Corinthians 6:18. Fortunately, this book is packed with suggestions on how women can arm themselves to be victorious and avoid the dangers that can so easily lead to destruction. This book acknowledges that "many have succumbed to the urgings of self," but it does a superb job of outlining the central elements of a more godly and satisfying strategy. For example, it suggests that two ways to deal with loneliness are to "deepen your relationship with God" and use that "as a springboard of service to others."

I hasten to add, in conclusion, that God's rules are as needed by men as by women. Every sexual act a single man has before marriage seems to deaden conscience cells in the brain and make the next sexual experience easier to enter into. God's call for chastity outside of marriage and fidelity within it—are like New Jersey barriers designed to protect all of us from oncoming traffic. By ignoring those barriers the Unites States has the world's highest rates of teen pregnancy, out-of-wedlock births and the world's highest divorce rate that breaks up half the new marriages.

There is a better way. As the authors quote Psalm 37:3-4

> Trust in the LORD and do good; dwell in the land and enjoy safe pasture. Delight yourself in the LORD and he will give you the desires of your heart.

Michael J. McManus
New York Times syndicated columnist
and author of *Marriage Savers: Helping Your Friends and Family Avoid Divorce*

Acknowledgments

*J*ust as Moses needed Aaron and Hur to support his arms as he watched over the battle between Israel and Amalek at Rephidim (Exodus 17:8-13), we have leaned heavily on many people, especially our husbands. Without their encouragement we would have failed to complete this project.

We thank the singles who took the time to fill out and return our questionnaire. Their input was a valuable resource.

We also thank Jon Graf, managing editor of *Discipleship Journal*, for reading the manuscript and making suggestions. Don E. Eberly, president of The Commonwealth Foundation and founder of the National Fatherhood Initiative, offered helpful remarks that enlarged our perspective of today's culture. Tom E. Smith, executive director of the Medical Institute for Sexual Health, provided resources and gave his time to ensure an accurate portrayal of sexually transmitted diseases. Sharon Benham, Deb Keating and Kris Mapstone contributed their insights. Debbie Krone, who graduated

from nursing school into heaven on March 9,
1996, also contributed her enthusiastic input.

Joy Jacobs
Deborah Strubel

Introduction

$\mathcal{U}$nmarried women are fighting a battle over sexual experience. Bombarded by the media and encouraged by the culture to believe that their peers are "enjoying the freedom" of sexual activity, many struggle with loneliness and rejection, feeling misunderstood.

While this book is a call to obey God's command prohibiting sexual intercourse outside of marriage, it is also an attempt to embrace with loving arms those struggling to uphold that command.

How exactly is one to go about remaining sexually pure while longing for a spouse? Is there any benefit to remaining a virgin when many other singles are not? What if one has already blown it sexually? How can forgiveness be found? Where is the strength to renew efforts toward chastity? Is there any hope if one has been violated by another against one's will?

Single women have shared their stories in this book in order to help the reader under-

1

stand that she is not alone. Their stories are true, although their names may have been omitted or changed, or details about them changed, to protect their identities.

The struggle to maintain sexual purity is a spiritual battle with unseen enemies. It is a battle fought in the mind, the will and the emotions. It is a battle that requires confession, repentance and a lifestyle of principle. It is a battle that requires sacrifice, but it promises reward in heaven and peace of mind here on earth.

This book deals with subjects that are difficult to verbalize, and inappropriate for male pastors or counselors to discuss in depth with women. It is therefore, a helpful resource for ministry leaders as well as for single women.

We have directed this book to women, not because men do not share the struggle for sexual purity, but because we are fulfilling the mandate in Titus 2:3-5: "The older women . . . can train the younger women to . . . be self-controlled and pure . . . so that no one will malign the word of God." Paul was referring to the people of the island of Crete, who were notorious for their lack of self-control. The contemporary parallel is obvious.

Maintaining or renewing sexual purity is a gift a single woman pours out to God and a gift she gives to a future spouse, if and when she has one, laying the foundation for a godly marriage.

Chapter 1

*P*remarital Sex and Culture

"*E*veryone thinks I'm so good! I feel like I ought to tell them the truth." An attractive female college student was in my office, struggling to overcome feelings of worthlessness after engaging in premarital sex.

I (Joy) put my hand on her arm to soften the blow of my question: "Diana, have you thought about being tested for AIDS?"

"We were *very* well protected." She grimaced. "*He* made sure of that."

Protected? I thought. *Protected from what?*

Besides the fact that condoms aren't even a reliable protection against pregnancy, what about protection from future thought patterns? From damaged emotions? What about protecting the wonder of God's gift of sex within marriage?

I knew Diana's sensitive conscience; the self-condemnation would hit her over and over again. She would also now have to fight the temptation to think, *I've already sinned once, so I might as well give in and do it again.*

Diana was in a war, waged on the battlefield of her mind. And she needed real protection. She needed to spiritually dress for the battle.

Sex Everywhere

Today's culture has reached the point where sex outside of marriage is expected. The "sexual revolution" of the 1960s has resulted in relaxed standards of sexual behavior, especially for women. According to the U.S. Centers for Disease Control and Prevention, in 1970 only 29 percent of females aged 15 to 19 had premarital sex. But by 1988, 51.5 percent had engaged in premarital sex. For 18-year-olds alone the figures for those years rose from 39 percent to 69 percent.[1]

The results of increased sexual activity are many. Many women, like Diana, struggle with guilt. Others report feelings of fear, anxiety, embarrassment and even disgust.

There are serious results for society as well, including rises in the number of sexually transmitted diseases, children born out of wedlock, abortions, and co-habitating couples. In 1991 there were 1.2 million out-of-wedlock births, meaning about one in every four children today is born to an unmarried mother.[2]

Eighty-two percent of women who had abortions in 1990 were unmarried.[3] In addition, the number of unmarried couples living together has skyrocketed from 523,000 in 1970 to 3,510,000 in 1993.[4]

Moments of stolen intimacy in the backseat of a car are a thing of the past. Sex between singles is performed in the spaciousness of a double bed while roommates watch television in the next room. A key issue in dating is no longer *if* one should have sex, but *when*. Many people feel that there is no reason to withhold the complete expression of sexual desires.

Singles today may believe that having sex before marriage will enable them to make better choices about compatible partners. Using this logic, nonvirgins should have more stable secure marriages than virgins. But Dr. Joan Kahn and Dr. Kathryn London found just the opposite effect when they studied U.S. women who were married between 1960 and 1985. "[W]omen who were sexually active prior to marriage faced a considerably higher risk of marital disruption than women who were virgin brides."[5]

Women who save themselves for an unknown future marriage partner watch as successions of eligible males drop them in favor of women who will "reward" them physically. Such women suffer ridicule from their peers and feelings of inadequacy from within.

Sexual Purity Has Rewards

Chastity is nothing to scoff at, however. "Sexual purity," says a single secretary, "is something to feel good about and should never make you feel that you've deprived yourself of something that everyone else is doing."

"God honors His word," a 51-year-old full-time Christian worker says, "and blessings always come out of obedience."

These women are right. The self-denial of today will translate into marital contentment and happiness tomorrow. A poll commissioned by the Family Research Council found 72 percent of those who were married and believed out-of-wedlock sex was wrong reported higher levels of sexual satisfaction than those who had little or no objection to sex outside marriage.

William Mattox, Vice President for policy at the Council, says the findings are consistent with the mid-1970s *Redbook* survey of 100,000 women. *Redbook* discovered that "women who were sexually active at age 15 were more likely to express dissatisfaction with their current sex lives than those who refrained from early sexual involvement." Women who had only one partner "experienced orgasm during sex more than twice as often as promiscuous women."[6]

Clearly, sexual purity has rewards that are seldom discussed today.

The Christian Battle

Of the 1,343 single Christians age 18 and older (703 who never married and 539 divorced persons) surveyed by Carolyn Koons and Michael Anthony, only 34 percent of the men and 41 percent of the women had chosen to refrain from sex while single. Twenty-two percent had lived with a member of the opposite sex on an intimate, unmarried basis. Of the sexually active, 35 percent of the men and 27 percent of the women admitted to having sex with four or more partners "as a single adult."[7] With the rise of AIDS and other sexually transmitted diseases, these statistics are frightening.

> *Single Christians who refrain from sex are in the minority.*

While not reaching the sexual involvement levels of non-Christians,[8] many Christians today are clearly struggling with how to remain sexually pure or renew chastity following divorce or widowhood. Many who are sexually active are having second thoughts about the "benefits" of sexual "freedom." And many who are not sexually active are experiencing emptiness and doubts.

Despite great mobility and personal freedom, singles today report their number one problem to be loneliness.[9] Both sexes worry about becoming self-centered.

According to *The Janus Report on Sexual Behavior*, fewer men and women today believe that their sexual practices should be in accord with their religion.[10] this is evidence that Christians today also tend to fit their religion into their lifestyle. Although they may pray and attend church, their religion has become compartmentalized. Sunday is for God, they think; the rest of the week is for doing what they like. When asked whom they consider the final authority to be, they answer, "me." Christians tend to do what seem easiest and most comfortable or most advantageous economically, regardless of whether or not it is biblically prudent.

Businessmen and author Patrick Morley says, "The American gospel has evolved into a gospel of addition without subtraction. It is the belief that we can add Christ to our lives, but not subtract us."[11]

By failing to maintain high moral standards, Christians have given Satan and his forces a stronghold from which to launch deeper, more devastating attacks. Such attacks can ignite a fire that threatens the very credibility not only of one person's relationship with God but of

Sexual sins threaten the very credibility not only of our personal relationship with God but the whole of Christianity

the whole of Christianity. When outward behavior fails to reveal the differences between professing Christians and non-Christians, Christianity is no longer a believable way of life. Unmarried Christians live together. Christians have children out of wedlock. Christians have affairs. Christians get divorced, Christian families are dissolved.

Defeated Christians are victories for Satan and his gang.

Satan knows that he's lost the war, but he doesn't give up on us. Through daily battles, he tries to keep us from realizing that we are God's *poiema*, God's workmanship (Ephesians 2:10). He wants us to be powerless, burdened and discouraged.

Christians cannot be ignorant of Satan's devices. We become a powerless people when we forget that we're a war! We must not forget that our enemy is Satan, not circumstances or other Christians. And we must know how to dress for daily battle and how to carry and use our weapons.

The Battle Has Begun

Spiritual warfare, as part and parcel of human experience, has been going on since Eve's initial skirmish with the serpent. After Adam's "pass the buck" explanation of his sin. Eve came up with the original "the devil made me do it" statement. God said this to the serpent: "And I will put enmity between you and the woman, and between your offspring and hers; he will crush your head, and you will strike his heel" (Genesis 3:15).

Using a variety of influences, from the media to pornography to the person in the next cubicle at work, "the god of this age," Satan, "has blinded the minds of unbelievers" (2 Corinthians 4:4). Men and women who believe in the supposed freedom of unrestrained sexual expression are actually prisoners of war, wearing masks provided by the enemy. The masks prevent them from acknowledging a battle they can't see, from recognizing their captive state and from trying to escape.

When a person repents, confesses his or her sin, trusts in Christ's redemptive power and submits to His lordship, the enemy becomes even more intent upon waging warfare against that person.

The struggle is not a physical one in the backseat of a car; it's spiritual wrestling that has been going on since mankind was created. It is the battle for who's in control: God or Satan.

But what chance is there to win a battle if we don't realize that a war is going on? If we don't know who the enemy is? If we wear shorts and sandals to battle? If we don't know how to use our weapons?

When Satan tempted Jesus (Luke 4:1-13), it was clear that the war was between two kingdoms. Satan, the commander-in-chief, "the ruler of the kingdom of the air" (Ephesians

2:2), controls the kingdom of darkness. His subjects gratify "the cravings of [the] sinful nature and [follow] its desires and thoughts" and so are "objects of [God's] wrath" (2:3).

God desires to rescue His children from the kingdom of darkness and bring them into the kingdom of light. Because God is "rich in mercy," He forgives their past and makes them "alive with Christ" (Ephesians 2:4-5). But He warns that as long as His subjects live on planet Earth, they are still in Adam and Eve's continuing battle.

As we live in this world, Satan and his forces continue to fight for control in a world we can't see by seeking to control the world we can see, including our society's laws, leaders and culture.

Sexual purity is a battle of the mind

Little support for sexual purity comes from today's laws or government leaders, although some circles have made calls for increased responsibility and sexual abstinence. No support for sexual purity exists in the media or popular culture. The major means of support must come from God.

Understanding the biblical standards of chaste behavior, feeling a God-given sense of guilt for not measuring up to those standards, confessing failures to the Lord and submitting behavior and thought patterns to Him will result in a changed world one person at a time.

A changed world begins with me . . . and you.

Where Did That Thought Come From?

The mind is the greatest battlefield in the struggle to overcome the influence of darkness and become like Christ. God's helmet of salvation protects the head or, more practically, the mind. Salvation in Christ is the first prerequisite to wholeness and holiness. Without that foundation we can go no further; with that foundation we can begin the process of renewing our minds, as God directs in Romans 12:2 (Amplified):

> *Our thought choices determine our feeling choices and our behavior choices.*

> . . . be transformed (changed) by the [entire] renewal of your mind—by its new ideals and its new attitude—so that you may prove [for yourselves] what is the good and acceptable and perfect will of God . . . [in His sight for you].

The question is: How do we renew our minds?

The Greek word *nous*—the conscious mind—is used in this passage. *Nous* is defined in Vine's *Expository Dictionary of New Testament Words* as "the seat of reflective consciousness, comprising the faculties of perception and understanding and those of feelings, judging, determining."

In other words, the *nous* is the part of us that makes conscious evaluations and decisions, including moral judgments. But although it's meant to control conscious thinking, our *nous* seems to have "a mind of its own." Some days we feel like we need to put a noose around our *nous* not to mention our emotions! How do we keep it all under control?

One of Satan's tactics is to deceive God's children into believing that their God-given potential can be realized under their own control, rather than under God's.

A song entitled "The Dilemma" explains the feeling that life is "a contradiction" with two lives warring inside and the "strong man" often winning the battle.

The apostle Paul expressed the same sentiment: "For I do not understand my own actions—I am baffled, bewildered. I do not practice *or* accomplish what I wish, but I do the very thing that I loathe [which my moral instinct condemns]" (Romans 7:15, Amplified).

How do we escape this dilemma? This statement from Dr. Larry Crabb, a Christian psychologist, is helpful: "How a person mentally *evaluates* an event determines how he *feels* about that event and how he will *behave* in response to it."[12]

We often think of the will of God for our lives as a 10- or 20-year plan, but it is actually fulfilled in what we could call "baby steps"—minute-to-minute decisions determining what we will or will not think about. These decisions may seem inconsequential at the time, but the reality is this: Our thought choices eventually determine our feeling choices and finally our behavior choices.

This process takes place in such a subtle way that feelings often overwhelm us and unexpected behavior overtakes us before we realize how powerful our wrong thought choices have been.

Ask yourself on a regular basis: Where are my thoughts coming from? From God? If not, where?

The mind is a battle zone. We are not just preparing *for* war, nor are we merely threatened *with* war. We are *at* war.

Satan plays with our heads. As A.W. Tozer said, we need to "talk back to the devil" and ask Jesus to show us the truth and keep us on target. In addition to wearing the helmet of salvation, we are to use the divinely empowered weapons discussed throughout the remainder of this book. These weapons demolish strongholds of thinking—"arguments and every pretension that sets itself up against the knowledge of God"—and "take captive every thought to make it obedient to Christ" (2 Corinthians 10:5).

In the early days of the Church, new converts were assigned two mentors: a catechist, who taught the basics of the faith, and an exorcist, who "tested the spirits." After the Age of Enlightenment, however, it became unacceptable to acknowledge a spiritual world with unseen spiritual beings.

This is another of Satan's strategies; after all, if we don't recognize the enemy, we can't fight him!

What Would Jesus Do?

Recently I (Joy) was talking with a senior saint, Reverend Ray Jarrett, a man who has held my respect and admiration for years. I described to him my lengthy struggle in making a decision and requested his prayer support.

There was a pause, and then the voice on the other end of the phone very kindly said, "Joy, I find that I don't have to make very many decisions anymore. I simply need to find the mind of Christ."

What a gentle but powerful admonishment! "Papa" Jarrett's quiet wisdom has come to mind over and over again in many different situations. It has a way of simplifying problematic decisions and, as my college editor used to say, stripping the issues "to the bone."

Charles Sheldon's classic, *In His Steps*, tells the story of a group of people of different occupations who covenanted before God to ask the question daily: What would Jesus do? Each member of the group, from a newspaper editor to a society debutante, found that life changed drastically in the face of this question.[13]

Is this a viable question in today's culture? Why not put it to the test? Try asking yourself these questions for a week (or, better yet, a month, since it takes 21 to 28 days to establish a habit): What would Jesus be thinking? How would Jesus react in this situation? What would Jesus do?

If Diana, from the illustration at the beginning of this chapter, had stopped to reflect on what Jesus would have done in her situation, she most likely would have been able to refrain from premarital sex.

Think about It:

1. Why does God prohibit sexual intimacy outside of marriage?

2. Why was abstaining from sexual immorality one of the three prohibitions decided upon by the Jerusalem church in Acts 15:19-21? What does that mean for Christians today?

3. How can understanding the mind of Christ help you refrain from sex?

Endnotes

1. U.S. Centers for Disease Control and Prevention. "Premarital Sexual Experience Among Adolescent Women—United States, 1970-1988," *Morbidity and Mortality Weekly Report* 39, nos. 51 & 52 (January 4, 1991), 929-932.

2. U.S. Bureau of the Census, *Statistical Abstract of the United States:* 1994 (114th ed.) Washington, DC, 1993, Tables 90 and 100.

3. Ibid., Table 112.

4. Ibid., Table 61.

5. Joan R. Kahn and Kathryn A. London, "Premarital Sex and the Risk of Divorce," *Journal of Marriage and the Family* 53 (November 1991), 845.

6. Quoted in William R. Mattrox Jr., "The Hottest Valentines," *The Washington Post*, February 1994.

7. Carolyn A. Koons and Michael J. Anthony, *Single Adult Passages: Uncharted Territories* (Grand Rapids, MI: Baker, 1991), 63, 68.

8. Only four percent of the single surveyed for the 1993 *Janus Report on Sexual Behavior* reported having no sexual partners. Forty percent had between 11 and 30 partners. Samuel S. Janus and Cynthia L. Janus, *The Janus Report on Sexual Behavior* (New York: John Wiley & Sons, Inc., 1993), 163.

9. Koons and Anthony, *Single Adult Passages*, 62, 67.

10. According to *The Janus Report* (p. 389), 50 percent of the people surveyed between 1983 and 1985 believed that it was important that their sexual practices were in harmony with their religion. Between 1988 and 1992, that figure was down to 35 percent of the men and 38 percent of the women. During that same period, those who felt that it was not important for their sexual practices to be in harmony with their religion increased from roughly 35 percent to about 42 percent.

11. Patrick M. Morley, *I Surrender: Submitting to Christ in the Details of Life* (Brentwood, TN: Wolgemuth and Hyatt, 1990), 14.
12. Lawrence A. Crabb, *Effective Biblical Counseling* (Grand Rapids, MI: Zondervan, 1977), 90.
13. Charles Sheldon, *In His Steps* (Uhrichsville, OH: The Christian Library, Barbour & Co., Inc., 1984).

Chapter 2

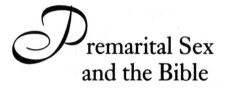

remarital Sex and the Bible

$\mathcal{C}$andy, a 30-year-old single, met Tony while vacationing with friends at a New Jersey beach. Tony lived in the area; Candy was several hours from home. They discovered that they enjoyed some of the same hobbies and were both churchgoers. Over dinner, they exchanged phone numbers.

Candy returned home feeling a warm glow of anticipation, but she spent a lot of time praying about what to do next. Having lost her virginity several years earlier, Candy had asked God to purify her life and renew her virginity. She was determined to take no chances. Tony invited her to return to the shore for the last big weekend of the season, but for several weeks Candy said no.

Tony's repeated phone calls finally caused Candy to relent, and on a Friday afternoon she drove east. After she arrived at her motel, she called Tony. They went out for dinner. The evening was filled with laughter and conversation, and Candy became even more attracted to Tony.

When they returned to her motel room, Tony asked if he could kiss her. She nodded, and Tony embraced her.

But his hug quickly became a powerful push toward the bed. One hand attempted to loosen her belt. Candy struggled. Before she got him out of her room, he had exposed himself to her.

Only through Candy's dedication to biblical standards of purity had she maintained her renewed virginity . . . but her glowing feelings had turned to cold shock.

To Abstain or Not to Abstain

Maintaining sexual purity has never been more difficult. Sexual abstinence while single, or after divorce or a spouse's death, or even after a one-night fling requires a conscious, deliberate act of the mind.

There are two ways you can lose virginity: You can consciously decide to experience sexual intercourse, or you can unconsciously decide to wait and see if there is a

> *A once-and-for-all decision about maintaining or renewing virginity acts as protection for the mind*

need to maintain sexual purity. Christian women, generally speaking, do not wake up in the morning and consciously decide, "Today I'm going to do all I can to experience sexual intercourse." Neither do they consciously plan at the onset of puberty to take steps to ensure that they are no longer virgins by the time they reach, say, age 20.

Rather, the majority of single women who are on the lookout for interesting male companionship believe that if and when they find that special someone, *then* they will think about how to deal with that companion's sexual advances and their own sexual arousal. To borrow the words of the investment company Dean Witter and apply them to the sexual arena, most Christians don't plan to fail; they fail to plan.

With the exception of the sexual abuse victim, loss of virginity follows *a decision to indulge* or *a decision not to decide*.

"I managed to keep my virginity until age 32, but unfortunately gave in to the overpowering urge of wanting to experience a sexual relationship," a single 36-year-old secretary said.

This woman wanted to experience sexual intercourse. She wanted to know if it was all that the world said it was. Her resolve was weakened by curiosity. Curiosity gave way to desire. Desire led her to complete the act. The Bible says it this way: "[B]ut each one is tempted when, by his own evil desire, he is dragged away and enticed. Then, after desire has conceived, it gives birth to sin" (James 1:14-15).

Reverend Neal Clarke, single and in his 50s, summed up the need for decision:

> [Sexual purity] is making some choices, up front, about your life, and settling them. That's easier said than done. A lot of people haven't done that. So every time they're in a potentially morally compromising situation, they go through the whole process again.
>
> I think it's got to happen way before that. Some decisions must be made in life as to what are the priorities . . . firm and fixed with God. In fact, I believe in making covenants with God. I think they keep you on target and give the Holy Spirit a hook.

The following passage is very definitive about the daily decisions—the "baby steps"—involved in finding the will of God for our lives:

> For *this is the will of God*, that you should be *consecrated—separated and set apart for pure and holy living: that you should abstain and* shrink from all sexual vice; That each one of you should know how to possess [*control, manage*] his own body (in purity. . .). Not [to be used] in the passion of lust.

. . . For God has not called us to impurity, but to consecration [to dedicate ourselves to the most thorough purity]. Therefore whoever disregards—sets aside and rejects this—disregards not man but God, Whose [very] Spirit [Whom] He gives to you [is] holy— chaste, pure. (1 Thessalonians 4:3-5, 7-8, Amplified, emphasis added)

In order that the Spirit of God may feel comfortable living in our bodies three factors are prerequisites to separation to God: (1) *consecration* of ourselves (mind, body, spirit); (2) *abstinence* from sexual sin; and (3) *control* of our appetites.

When we ask the questions presented earlier—what would Jesus be thinking? How would Jesus react? What would Jesus do?—in relation to chastity, we soon realize that although we usually think of virginity in a physical sense, we must also think in terms of *spiritual and mental virginity*.

Decisions in today's world require the innocence (which some may mistakenly term ignorance) of a physically virginal teenager named Mary, who asked, in response to Gabriel's announcement of her impending pregnancy, "How can this be?"

Her question reflected a virginal "Mary mind." Gabriel assured Mary that God's power would enable the impossible to take place, and Mary's final reply to the voice of God was the pure outflow of a "Mary mind": "Be it done to me according to your word" (Luke 1:38, NASB).

You might ask about a totally different situation: "How can this be? How can God use me in this way when I have had no experience in this area?"

Finding the will of God for my life requires that I am willing for my little world to change. Willing for my faith to be stretched. Willing for my ways of thinking and reacting to be extended outside the confining limits within which they have comfortably rested.

Understanding the Value of Virginity

The culture of biblical times demanded virginity in a bride; furthermore, women in Mary's day knew that virginity was a prerequisite for becoming the mother of the Messiah. That hope may have kept some young women pure. But what about today?

Reverend Jack Hayford gives 10 reasons for the high value of virginity, all of which are applicable today:

1. It honors the wisdom of the Creator's design and order.

2. It is the symbol of an exclusive allegiance to Jesus Christ.

3. It prizes purity as a precious treasure to be preserved and protected.

4. It rejects the mockery which treats innocence as though it were ignorance.

5. It retains for a single beloved one what appropriately is theirs.

6. It refuses the notion that love and relationship require sexual expression for fulfillment.

7. It gains dominion over sensuality, thus opening the possibility of highest sensual fulfillment.

8. It repels the attempted invasion of the soul, which lost chastity allows.

9. It walks a pathway which avoids contracting other polluting traits of a decaying world.

10. It exercises a self-control, which sustains a fuller sense of self-worth. (The life isn't sold off cheaply.)[1]

Recent studies also show that saving sex for marriage leads to higher levels of sexual satisfaction once marriage takes place. Sexual satisfaction, in turn, contributes to marital satisfaction.

The first year of marriage is often filled with strife. Discovering the wonder and closeness of the sex act provides a new couple with a powerful urge to solve their disagreements.

"Our first year of marriage," Tonya said, "we fought about everything. Toothpaste, bathrobes, toilet seats . . . stupid stuff. Sometimes we had to stay up really late so we wouldn't go to bed angry. No one ever slept on the couch. Sex was our new marriage toy, and it gave us a reason to make up."

> *God provides the weapons of salvation, righteousness, truth, peace, faith, Scripture and prayer to enable us to prevent Satan from gaining a stronghold in our lives or demolish a stronghold he has already established*

Do you want to have a higher likelihood of being happy in marriage? Save sex until after the ceremony.

The Value of Renewed Virginity

If you are no longer a virgin, you may believe that there is no reason to resist continued sexual expression. This is where Satan has built a stronghold, a fortress, in your life. From here he turns up the heat of the battle another notch. True, you will never be able to deny the fact of that first sexual experience. True, you will never again be able to think of yourself as a virgin. But all is not lost, as Satan would have you think.

The sense of self-control, the ability to keep your bodily passions in check and the knowledge that you are daily obeying God's commands are benefits that you can derive from beginning today to abstain from further sexual experience.

In medieval times, before the invention of gunpowder and cannons, fortresses were almost impossible to penetrate. The best way to defeat the inhabitants of a castle was to surround it and cut it off from receiving supplies, particularly food, from the outside. The attackers then waited for the inhabitants to die of disease or starve to death. Sometimes, if the attacking army wanted to speed up death by disease, they used a catapult to hurl animal carcasses over the castle walls.

This isolation strategy is the one to use on Satan's fortress in your life. First, surround the fortress by recognizing Satan's ally: sex. Determine to starve those awakened sexual desires out of existence. Exercise self-control by keeping your bodily passions, including thoughts and fantasies, under God's control. Exercise self-control by ridding yourself of those companions who cause defeat. Deny yourself, and keep on denying yourself.

Speed up the process by introducing a little "disease" for Satan's gang: Read and memorize Scripture; pray without ceasing. "Resist the devil, and he will flee from you" (James 4:7).

Each time you resist any of the daggers the dark forces throw at you, you increase your spiritual muscle and gain ability to fight further attacks.

You can say no to sex. You can begin today. Renewing your virginity means making the conscious decision to refrain from continued sex outside of marriage and then following through with proper behavior choices.

Consider making a covenant with God to maintain or renew your virginity.

Covenant with God

Reverend Clarke, a pastor and district superintendent, considered ministry choices more important than marriage choices. In his case, that has resulted in remaining single. Each marital state has its own benefits . . . its own responsibilities . . . its own temptations. It has not been an easy choice for Reverend Clarke. A covenant with God cannot be taken lightly.

In today's world, it is difficult to understand the true weight of covenant agreement. A covenant is not a contract: A contract involves limited liability, but a covenant involves unlimited liability.

A covenant means death to independent living. It is an agreement in which the partners are willing to lay down their lives for each other. The life shared between them becomes the priority.

Marriage is an example of such a covenant. But singles are not without a covenant simply because they are unmarried. All believers covenant with Christ on the day they receive His gift of salvation.

Covenants between God and man reveal God's perfect will and purpose for man and reflect God's love, grace and mercy. Jesus "gave himself for our sins to rescue us from the present evil age, according to the will of our God and Father" (Galatians 1:4).

Singles can reflect God's love, grace and mercy by being living sacrifices to Him. One essential sacrifice is the laying down of sexual desires.

Christians may not always be faithful in covenant, but God is: " 'Though the mountains be shaken and the hills be removed, yet my unfailing love for you will not be shaken nor my covenant of peace be removed,' says the Lord, who has compassion on you" (Isaiah 54:10). Christians may fall into sexual sin—fornication (sex between unmarried persons) or adultery (sex between persons who are married to others). But God is faithful.

God desires to enable us to keep covenant: "But thanks be to God, who always leads us in triumphal procession in Christ and through us spreads everywhere the fragrance of the knowledge of him. For we are to God the aroma of Christ" (2 Corinthians 2:14-15).

But non-Christians will not appreciate the terms of our covenant: "For we are to God the aroma of Christ among those who are being saved and those who are perishing. To the one we are the smell of death; to the other, the fragrance of life" (2:15-16).

Strength in keeping covenant does not come from the approval of others, but from acceptance by God:

> [Y]ou are a letter from Christ . . . written not with ink but with the Spirit of the living God, not on tablets of stone but on tablets of human hearts.
>
> Such confidence as this is ours through Christ before God. Not that we are competent in ourselves to claim anything for ourselves, but our *competence comes from God*. He has made us competent as ministers of a *new covenant*—not of the letter but of the Spirit; for the letter kills, but the Spirit gives life. (2 Corinthians 3:3-6, emphasis added)

Since Christians are a letter from Christ, imagine how confusing the contents are if we exhibit unrestrained sexual practices which are contrary to God's Word. Any message of eternal hope that we wish to proclaim to others becomes lost when our lives and ethics look much the same as those of our neighbors.

God's strength can enable Christians to keep covenant through the loneliest of times. Through those lonely times, times of heartache and trial, others to whom we wish to proclaim Christ will see that we are indeed different.

The apostle Paul's times of imprisonment are good examples of this. During Paul's first imprisonment in Rome, he lived in a rented house, and his surroundings were reasonably pleasant. When he wrote his second letter to Timothy, however, he was chained like a common criminal in a cold dungeon.

But his tone was triumphant:

> I know whom I have believed, and am convinced that he is able to guard what I have entrusted to him for that day.
> What you heard from me, keep as the pattern of sound teaching, with faith and love in Christ Jesus. (2 Timothy 1:12-13)

Then Paul added, "You know that everyone in the province of Asia has deserted me" (2 Timothy 1:15). Probably one of Paul's reasons for writing Timothy was his loneliness: "I long to see you" (2 Timothy 1:4).

Earlier in his life, Paul had made the choice to remain single. (Some Bible scholars believe that Paul was a widower because he had been a member of the Sanhedrin, and to be a member of that ruling body one had to be married.) The choice of singleness would have given Paul the freedom to follow God's will, wherever his missionary journeys led him.

Accept Singleness As a Gift—for Today or Tomorrow

Perhaps you are single not by choice, but through lack of quality marriage prospects, an unwanted divorce or the death of your spouse. "Singleness is important for every woman to consider because at some point in her adult life every woman is likely to be single for a time because of the high divorce rate and the different life-spans of men and women."[2]

In Paul's famous treatise on the subject in First Corinthians, he points out that single and married persons are equal before God. Each person must determine in her own mind what state is God's will for her. Paul says, "[E]ach one should retain the place in life that the Lord assigned to him and to which God has called him" (7:17). In other words, accept the situation in which you find yourself. Accept singleness as a gift from God.

Right! you are thinking. *Easier said than done.*

Does accepting singleness as a gift make sense? Every person comes into the world single, and all will exit this world alone. Married persons may try to blame their spouses for their sins or attempt to ride the coattails of a saintly partner into heaven, but each person will stand before God, alone.

We are each responsible for our own iniquity. Conversely, each one of us is gifted with our own "uniquity."

God created Adam and initially put him in the garden *alone*, telling him to "work it and take care of [cultivate] it" (Genesis 2:15). This happened *before* God created Eve and brought Adam and Eve together.

> *As Corrie ten Boom's life exemplifies, accepting singleness as a gift from God can turn your hurts into a heavenly love*

Does this mean that God intended for men and women to understand their calling (their life's work) and to cultivate their surroundings and themselves, through preparation and education, before they come together in marriage? It may be stretching the point to make the creation story allegorical, but working at finding our "uniquity" before marriage, if and when it occurs, is certainly a very healthy move.

Corrie ten Boom, whom Billy Graham has described as "one of the most amazing lives of the century,"[3] did not choose singleness. Her biographer, Joan Winmill Brown, tells how Corrie's "first encounter with dying to self became a focal point of her adult commitment to Christ . . . through the door of a broken heart."[4]

At the tender age of 14, Corrie fell in love with Karel, a handsome ministerial student. As she matured to womanhood, Karel's interest in her grew. But Karel's parents expected him to "marry well," and so the courtship ended.

Corrie, however, refused to give up her dream, until the day Karel said, "Corrie, I want you to meet my fiancée!"

Through wise words from her earthly father, Corrie was able to turn to her heavenly Father. When blocked love causes pain, her father said, you have two choices: Either kill the love, or ask Christ to help you change your love to a heavenly kind of love.

Corrie surrendered to the Lord her longing for marriage and her wounded heart. Although her internal struggle was fierce, God gave her victory and peace. Corrie said, "I never brought a child to birth, but I thank the Lord for using me to bring some to rebirth. That is the greatest joy for a Christian. Perhaps this was a bit of losing my life for Jesus and therefore winning it."[5]

"Joe's" Story

Even though his family had rejected him, "Joe" accepted God's authority in his life and committed himself to making decisions that honored God. Instead of wasting time ruminating bitterly over past injustices, he worked hard and eventually made his employer very successful.

His hard work didn't go unnoticed especially by his boss's wife, who found "Joe" very attractive. Her seduction was anything but subtle: "Come to bed with me!"

"Joe" stopped to think. After all, life had been unfair to him. He had experienced a lot of bad breaks. His boss seemed to take his hard work for granted, and his boss's wife certainly was alluring. Besides, who would ever know? She wasn't going to tell her husband . . .

Wrong! You know "Joe" as Joseph, an Old Testament character whose choice had already been made. His covenant with God had already been established. Genesis 39:8 states emphatically, "He refused"!

Joseph said, "How then could I do such a wicked thing and sin against God?" Joseph's mind was already made up. His covenant with God had been established. He was wearing the *helmet* that protected his thinking and behavior.

And although Potiphar's seductive wife spoke to Joseph day after day, he refused to go to bed with her or even be with her. But she didn't give up.

One day when Joseph went to work, none of the household servants were around. Unexpectedly, he found himself alone with Mrs. Potiphar. She had dismissed the servants, filled the air with erotic fragrances and spent the early hours of the day preparing her face and body for this encounter.

She grabbed his shirt, looked into his eyes and left nothing to the imagination with her bold words of invitation: "Come to bed with me!"

Well, Joseph had been chaste—and chased!—for a long time. His alarm hadn't gone off that morning; in his hurry to get to work on time, he had missed his quiet time with God, and he was feeling very lonely, discouraged and vulnerable. He couldn't be nasty to his boss's wife or he might lose his job, so he decided to sit down and talk with her about their relationship and where it was headed.

Wrong again! Joseph didn't allow himself to stay in a situation that he couldn't handle. He was wearing the helmet that protected his thinking. His decision had already been made.

He left his cloak in her hand and ran out of the house.

Potiphar's peeved wife lied about him and Joseph ended up in jail. Sometimes we're not rewarded when we do the right thing. Or at least it doesn't seem that way at the time.

Planning to Fail or Failing to Plan?

You will face situations different from the one Joseph faced, but right patterns of thinking lead to right decisions and actions.

Compare Joseph's story with "Sam's."

"Sam" had made all the vows of "the separated life," but "Sam" paid only lip service to those vows; he had not personally made a covenant with God. He saw no immediate benefit in keeping his vows, and he did whatever felt good at the time.

But it didn't feel good when "Sam" (his full name was Samson) pulled down the pillars of a pagan temple around his "incredible hulk" of a body. Probably his demise came as no great surprise to those who knew him because, despite his amazing physical strength, his life had already been in ruins for years.

A conscious, deliberate act of the mind—knowing the Commander-in-Chief's rules for battle and covenanting to obey those rules—is a necessary prerequisite to sexual purity.

Think about It:

1. Can you express why you wish to remain a virgin or renew sexual abstinence? Put your thoughts in writing, in the form of a purpose statement.

2. Base your purpose statement on Scripture. (Suggested verses: 1 Corinthians 6:13-17, 10:8; Ephesians 5:3; 1 Thessalonians 4:3-8.)

3. What, specifically, do you need to do in order to starve Satan out of any strongholds he might have in your life?

4. The Bible says that your life is like a letter from God to the world. What does your letter say?

Endnotes

1. Reverend Jack Hayford, quoted from program #3433 (Living Way Ministries, Ambassador Advertising Agency, 515 East Commonwealth Ave., Fullerton, CA 92632; 714-738-1510; 1994).
2. Jim and Sally Conway, *Women in Mid-Life Crisis* (Wheaton, IL: Tyndale, 1983), 61.
3. Joan Winmill Brown, *Corrie: The Lives She's Touched* (Old Tappan, NJ: Fleming H. Revell Co., 1979), 11.
4. Ibid., 19.
5. Ibid., 20.

Chapter 3

For Those Who Have Sinned

I (Deb) was lying flat on my back, halfway around the world from everyone I knew and loved. I had come to Australia as a short-term missionary intending to serve others. Instead "the others" had to serve me: I had a severe case of mononucleosis.

I was so sick that when my arm rested on my abdomen, the weight of the arm caused pain on my stomach. But I was too tired to move my arm. I would lie there in agony as I mentally coached myself: "I must move my arm. Oh, I can't. I must move my arm. Let me just rest a little more, and then I'll move it. Oh, it hurts. How my stomach hurts." Finally, with a great effort, I would summon the strength to slide my arm over an inch or two until it fell off my abdomen and onto the bed.

Lying there, I could do nothing but think and pray. I could commune with no one but God. Occasionally a gecko would climb the block wall beside my bed, and I would thank God for the diversion.

Scenes and voices of childhood came to mind. Hurts rolled over me. With no one to hear, I cried freely for hours.

Deep down inside, under the well-camouflaged layers of defense, cowered a little girl who longed to be loved by a man, who longed to be married. I had never admitted that to myself before.

I thought that I was ruined for life as a result of my parents' unhappy marriage. How would I ever be able to know what love meant? How could I even dream of establishing a good relationship with a man, let alone hope for a decent marriage? A great marriage was certainly out of the question, I was sure of that. "But God," I begged, "is asking for an adequate marriage too much?"

Recognize that feelings from your past can have a powerful impact on your present sexual tendencies

God showed me that I was bitter. I was unforgiving. I was full of anger. Oh, I had neatly covered over those emotions. Anyone who knew me assumed by my demeanor that I was mild-mannered and totally agreeable. I remember telling an acquaintance during our first real conversation, "I hardly ever get angry."

His discerning reply startled me: "You get angry. You just don't know it. In fact, you're angry almost all the time." How could a relative stranger know me better than I knew myself?

God gave me the strength to release family members who had hurt me. I wanted to stay angry. I wanted to punish them by my anger. Instead of punishing them, my bitterness and

Forgive those who have hurt you

my furious search for love and my lack of sexual boundaries were ruining my life.

God showed me that He had forgiven me. I did not deserve His mercy. I deserved His condemnation. Yet He loved me. He loved me enough to die for me. On what basis then could I refuse to forgive others?

And He was promising to be my Father, to give me the love I so desperately craved. "Yes, Lord," I said reluctantly, "be my Daddy. Teach me about love, how to receive it and how to give it."

I'd like to say that I returned home and lived happily ever after. However, I still didn't have the courage to say no when I needed to or to break off the parasitic relationship in which I was involved. It took several months of continued physical clinging and fawning until I was able to walk, away from the man in my life.

An entry from my journal reflects my hurt and fear:

> We sat there in the car staring blankly at the reflections on the river. Physical space as well as emotional distance separated us. "I'm a perfectionist," he said. "Even if you were the queen of England, you still wouldn't please me."
>
> I said, "That's okay," then turned and ran up the steps as my quiet suppressed sobs turned into big sad tears. By the time I had run blindly up three flights of stairs and unlocked my door, the dam had burst. I had sacrificed my self-respect in order to gain his approval, and when it was all said and done, I hadn't even succeeded in doing that.

In the time following that experience I became willing to remain single, if that was God's wish. I still had hopes of being married, but at the same time I somehow dreaded it. I had observed so many unhappy marriages that I couldn't bring myself to expect anything better.

Those events took place over 15 years ago. Since then God has blessed me exceedingly more than I ever hoped or dreamed although, because I learned some lessons slowly, I still encountered some difficult experiences.

My next relationships were more healthy because I was depending on God, not my boyfriend, to meet my needs. Sex, however, remained a continuous source of struggle and temptation, because once appetites are whetted and then indulged, they become very powerful. It is a struggle, the remnants of which I must deal with to this day—not because God isn't powerful, but because I am weak.

Sometimes even scripturally based thinking and decisions are clouded or influenced by emotions left over from past experiences. Old feelings of failure and worthlessness or worries about normalcy come crowding in.

And that may happen quite unexpectedly to you. You can prepare for those times by acknowledging and examining your vulnerable areas now.

Circumstances surrounding your childhood may provide clues to understanding and expelling any feelings of worthlessness. Past hurts may have made you extra sensitive in certain areas. Many adults have been wounded emotionally in childhood and bear the scars of a poor or nonexistent father/child relationship.

Effects of Father Absence

David Blankenhorn, a leading expert on the effects of father absence on individuals and society, has written and spoken extensively on the subject. "Scholars estimate that, before they reach age eighteen, more than half of all children in the nation will live apart from their fathers for at least a significant portion of their childhoods."[1]

While the Christian community is usually five to seven years behind the rest of society in most general trends, more and more Christian families have experienced, and will continue to experience, the tragedy of divorce.

Adults who grew up in Christian homes where divorce was considered unacceptable may have witnessed emotional or physical abuse between their parents or may have had fathers who simply escaped into the work or church leadership worlds.

What are the effects of father absence?

For girls, as well as some boys, the effects of fatherlessness show up in adolescence as problems in forming intimate relationships. Daughters of widows may tend toward shyness and inhibition with men. Daughters of divorced women may become sexually promiscuous, because they might think, "What do I need to do, and who do I need to be, to find a man who won't abandon me, as the men in my life and my mother's life have done?"[2]

Sex is often used as an aphrodisiac in a desperate search for love and acceptance. The "party girl" may fly from one relationship directly into another with no thought about the types of partners she has chosen or why each relationship comes to a dissatisfying end. She may stay in a bad relationship because it seems preferable to being alone. The deeply hidden fear remains: Perhaps I am unlovable.

For boys, problems caused by lack of an involved father are more complex and may begin before adolescence. As they grow, "boys seek to separate from their mothers in search of the meaning of their maleness."[3] The father shows his son that he also can be a man. If the boy cannot separate from his mother and learn to be the son of his father, one result, according to Blankenhorn, is rage—extreme anger against mother, women and society. This rage is manifested in violence and lawlessness.

Another result, says Blankenhorn, is hypermasculinity, or the "need to prove their manhood all by themselves, without the help of fathers."[4] This manifestation may lead to wanting to conquer women, trying to impregnate women or committing rape and violence.

An additional result of the absent father can be homosexuality. In a family with a domineering mother and an absent or passive father, a boy may be drawn to stronger, more aggressive youths who inspire his admiration.[5] Particularly if the mother makes one male child her confidant, that child becomes, in an emotional sense, her husband, whom she subtly teaches to acquire the traits she misses in her distant or absent husband. The child then can never comfortably oppose her, or separate from her, in order to learn masculine traits.[6]

Effects of Parental Apathy

What about children who receive little or no physical touch or affection from either parent?

Harri became very good at rationalizing. For a long time she justified her homosexual activity because of the lack of affection, both verbal and physical, in her family. How she had longed for touch and time from her parents, but they were always too busy with the print shop! And all the kids were expected to help out in the family business, whether they had any natural ability or not.

As Harri's resentment grew, she spent increasing amounts of time away from home, usually with several girlfriends. When she was away from home, not only did she avoid having to work, but she also avoided having to think about why her parents practically ignored her. Gradually, as she left her friends' apartments, goodbye hugs lengthened. Eventually the hugs started earlier in the evening.

As a lonely teenager, Harri was hooked . . . for a while. Through an extremely embarrassing situation, separation from her friends during her college years and understanding from a woman counselor, Harri was finally able to recognize and fulfill her true needs—not for sexual involvement, but for physical touch and affection from people who cared about her.

Anthropologist Ashley Montagu, who has studied the significance of touch in various cultures, maintains that the Western world's "frenetic preoccupation with sex . . . is . . . not the expression of sexual interest . . . but rather a search for the satisfaction of the need for contact." If a child receives inadequate touching, he or she becomes physically and psychologically awkward with others. Montagu found that frequent physical contact received later in life may relieve current stress and tension; it has also produced dramatic breakthroughs in formerly unreachable schizophrenics, autistic children and even a severe asthmatic.[7]

One divorced woman who appreciated the reassuring effects of touch regularly greeted her women friends with a hug. "We're having a hugging party," she'd tell bystanders. "Everybody can use a hug."

Nonsexual touching and hugging are more socially acceptable within some Christian churches than others. Some outsiders who are thrust into such touch-oriented churches may feel threatened or mistakenly perceive some underlying sexual connotation, while

Allow God to be your Father

others find that these churches fulfill their need to connect with others.

You can experience another form of touch therapy by buying a rocking chair and using it regularly. Hey, it's okay—when your friends come to take you to the nursing home, tell them that you're just trying a theory you read about in a book! Or how about swinging on the swings in the park? The feel of the air against your skin can be a caress from God.

The Cure

Where can this generation of fatherless children find help? If you recognize your family in any of the above scenarios, are you doomed? Where can you find comfort if your parents were uninvolved or unaffectionate?

Quite naturally, the secular world believes that fatherlessness "cannot really be remedied." It cannot be offset by a hard-working, more involved mother or by more social programs. "We will solve it only with fathers."[8] And they are right in terms of the resources of this world.

"I will be a Father to you, and you will be my sons and daughters, says the Lord Almighty" (2 Corinthians 6:18).

God stands ready to be your Father. You can call Him "Abba," "Daddy." He will never abandon you. He is always concerned about you. You can and must commit your entire being to Him, not just with your head but with your heart.

Larry Crabb points to two keys that are essential if we are ever to live godly, fulfilled lives: "the security of being truly loved and accepted, and the significance of making a substantial, lasting, positive impact on another person."⁹

These two needs must be understood and resolved before we can live the righteous life God intends. Crabb points out that without resolution of these issues, we attempt to manipulate others, such as our spouses or friends, into ministering to us.

We do not need to feel secure or significant to be godly, but we must understand and believe that Christ has made us secure and significant. A right view of God always precedes a right view of ourselves. When we have confidence in God as our Source of security and significance, then we are free to minister to others in true Christlike form. Our relationships take on healthy characteristics of mutual giving and commitment.

Facing the Facts

How about your past? Are there skeletons of sin buried under the boxes of old books or shoes in your closet?

While an unmarried woman may feel loved prior to and during the sex act, she most certainly (provided she is honest with herself) feels unloved and used after the liaison is over or the partner has gone off with a new lover.

> *"Casual sex" is a contradiction in terms*

"It can leave you feeling very cheap and used when it's all over," a 36-year-old single woman said. "You lose a lot of self-respect when you surrender your virginity at the wrong time."

"Certain men," a 30-year-old divorced saleswoman said, "can have a sexual experience without emotional commitment, and then walk away . . . often leaving the woman feeling disappointed in herself and angry at the man."

In the movie *Indecent Proposal*, Demi Moore and Woody Harrelson play a married couple who are very committed to each other. Robert Redford offers the couple a million dollars if Demi will spend one night with him.

They struggle over this decision. Demi finally says, "Hey, all I'm going to give him is my body. I'm not going to give him my mind or my heart."

"You can't do it!" says Jim Dethmer, author of *The Best-Kept Secret about Sex*. "It's an axiomatic law of the universe." He goes on to say that "sex is . . . an intimate, permanent connection between maleness and femaleness that is irrevocable, that leaves a part of ourself someplace else." He says that sex outside of marriage is like sticking your wet tongue on a freezing metal pipe and then removing it.[10] Ouch!

Forgiveness in Christ

"The body is not meant for sexual immorality, but for the Lord, and the Lord for the body" (1 Corinthians 6:13). Some of us have found this out the hard way, through experience. We feel dirty and used. In addition to feeling unloved by someone in this world, we feel tremendous guilt. We *feel* guilty because we *are* guilty.

"Do you not know that your body is a temple of the Holy Spirit, who is in you, whom you have received from God? You are not your own; you were bought at a price" (6:19-20). The good news is that the price for our sin has been

> *Determine to show your gratitude to Christ by renewing your efforts to be chaste*

paid by Christ's blood. By paying that price, He has bought us.

Imagine yourself as a slave—not because of your skin color, as in pre-Civil War days, but because of your sin. Your deeds and your guilt have pronounced you a slave.

Imagine that you are standing on the auction platform. Bidders are examining the goods. When the auctioneer starts, no one bids for you. Your price drops lower and lower. Potential buyers don't bid; they just walk away.

Exasperated, the auctioneer finally offers you to what's left of the crowd—free. You feel the abject humiliation of being unwanted, even at that price.

Then a stranger dressed in white appears. He heaves bag after bag, filled with gold nuggets earned by his sweat and blood, onto the auctioneer's stand.

"I want her for my wife," he says, looking at you with love.

By now a crowd has gathered. They stand in shocked silence and stare as the stranger removes his fine white coat and places it gently around you.

"You are no longer a slave," he says. "You have been bought with a price. Therefore honor God with your body."

We who have committed sins against God and our own bodies are that slave. The stranger is our Lord and Savior, who has paid an exorbitant price to redeem us.

Once we realize that our sexual sins have been forgiven, what remains is the choice of how we will show our gratitude to the One who has bought us. "Go now," Jesus declares, "and leave your life of sin" (John 8:11).

Surrender Total Self to God

What a wonderfully expansive feeling Sue had while flying to Europe, free at last from the claustrophobic confines of her strict Christian upbringing and the legalism of the Christian college she had attended. She determined to leave her goody-goody image on the western shores of the Atlantic.

She and her friend, Katie, were lounging in the gardens outside the Museum of Modern Art in Rome when two handsome Italian men began chatting with them. The foursome spent the afternoon together and agreed to meet later that evening for a night on the town.

After drinks at several cafés that evening, Sue knew that her male friend was interested in only one thing: sex. For three hours she beat off his advances, until he gave up and slumped off into the night.

Unfortunately Katie was enjoying her partner, leaving Sue feeling very awkward. As they finally hurried to catch the last train out of the subway station, Sue looked forward to relaxing in her hotel room.

To her surprise, they arrived not at their hotel, but at the apartment of the Italian man. Here Sue was introduced to his male roommate.

Confess your sexual sins to the Lord; ask God to reveal other sin patterns to you

As it was now early morning, all of the subways and buses had stopped running. And Sue was out of Italian cash, so she couldn't call a cab. They had traveled for what seemed like forever, so she knew she couldn't walk. Even though she was a tourist, she could tell that this was a bad section of Rome. She was trapped.

She peered around the apartment, which consisted of only one room. A large double bed hugged one wall. A row of kitchen cabinets and tiny appliances lined the opposite wall. A table with two chairs stood in front of a sofabed. Four people could squeeze around the table if two of them sat on the bed.

The two men motioned Sue and Katie aside, and they unfolded the sofabed into the only remaining space. They peeled off one of the blankets from the double bed and threw it on the sofabed. Sue figured she'd sleep with Katie. No problem.

While Sue removed her shoes and tried to figure out a discreet way to slip off her dress and slide into bed, she heard a rustle and a giggle. Turning her head, she caught a glimpse of Katie slipping under the cover of the double bed into the arms of her male friend.

They turned off the light. The roommate lay on the sofabed staring at Sue. And Sue sat on the foot of the sofabed, sobbing. It wasn't supposed to happen like this. She wanted to be in love the first time it happened.

Sue's inner desire to taste the "delights" of sin led her into companionship with a friend who exhibited no sexual boundaries and finally ended in a compromising situation. She could confess her one night of sin, but to be truly repentant she would also need to confess her inner rebellion against not only her parents, but also God's Word.

For those of us who have willfully transgressed, we need to submit our whole being to God's authority, not just plead forgiveness for our sexual sins in order to be successful in renewing a vow of chastity.

Walter Trobisch writes, "In cleaning up the mess, don't stop with the sex corner, but clean up the other dark corners as well." Confess other sins or sin patterns in your life. "It may well be that the cause of your failures and defeats in the realm of sex is compromise and disobedience in other areas of life where you disregarded the will of God."[11]

The key to godliness in all areas of life is that our consciences be "enlightened, instructed, purged, and kept clean."[12] This requires exposing and enslaving our consciences to God's Word. A good conscience can be our greatest blessing and a bad one our greatest foe.

It doesn't matter whether we feel fatherless, or feel secure, or feel loved; we can know true love. We can experience the love of a father through God, our heavenly Father. Understanding and believing that God provides the only sure security in this world of uncertainty will enable us to place our admiration, our praise and our trust solely in Him.

God does remove the desire for sex from some single Christians who were formerly bound by sexual sin. For others God chooses to allow temptation again and again. Repeated temptations toward the same sin are to test our faithfulness to God and our willingness to lean solely on Him. When we acknowledge and understand our weak areas, we can call on God's strength to help us.

Think about It:

1. Has your need to belong driven you into undesirable relationships? If so, what should you do with those relationships?

2. Has your need to belong caused you to rebel against your family or your lack of family?

3. Are you trying to fill the father-shaped need in your life through harmful relationships?

4. Jesus called God "Abba," the Hebrew word easiest to pronounce for a child who is just learning to speak. Are you trying to fill the God-shaped vacuum in your life through human relationships? How can you allow God to be your "Daddy"?

5. What other sin areas need to be yielded to "Abba," Father? How can you become more wholly accountable to Him, knowing that He desires the very best for you?

6. Through Jesus' atonement for sins, we are made acceptable in the eyes of His holiness. This is your Father's gift to you: the

"breastplate of righteousness." How does being accepted by God protect you?

Endnotes

1. David Blankenhorn, *Fatherless America* (New York: Basic Books, 1995), 18.
2. Judith Musick, quoted in Blankenhorn, *Fatherless America*, 47.
3. Ibid., 30.
4. Ibid., 31.
5. John White, *Eros Defiled* (Downers Grove, IL: InterVarsity Press, 1977), 115.
6. Ibid.
7. Ashley Montagu, *Touching: The Human Significance of the Skin* (New York and London: Columbia University Press, 1971), 167, 212-213, 218.
8. Blankenhorn, *Fatherless America*, 47-48.
9. Lawrence J. Crabb Jr., *The Marriage Builder* (Grand Rapids, MI: Zondervan, 1982), 20.
10. Quoted in *The Christian Reader*; from *Preaching Today*, Tape 128 (Willow Creek Association, 1994).
11. Walter Trobisch, *Love Is a Feeling to Be Learned* (Downers Grove, IL: InterVarsity Press, 1971), 36-37.
12. J.I. Packer, *A Quest for Godliness: The Puritan Vision of the Christian Life* (Wheaton, IL: Crossway Books, 1990), 107.

Chapter 4

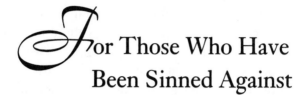

For Those Who Have Been Sinned Against

Part of knowing ourselves may require facing the fact of past sexual abuse. How does that tie into what may seem to be the "impossible dream" of sexual purity?

Jill, a college junior with long auburn curls and the body of a model, came to me (Joy) for counseling for suicidal depression. She described her relationship with a lover who was uncommitted to her, the trauma of the sexually transmitted disease she had contracted and her sense of hopelessness because of the Human Papilloma virus which, her doctor told her, will be with her permanently.

Finally, Jill expressed her feeling toward the man who had used her. Was she angry at him? No. She saw the problem as a deficiency in herself. "I just don't understand why he couldn't fall in love with me."

Her statement was a red flag that immediately signaled me to ask, "Jill, were you sexually abused as a child?" The answer, as I expected, was positive. Her lack of self-worth gave it away.

Then there was Hope, a young mother of two little girls. Hope had been sexually abused by her father from an early age. Her mother had been abusive as well, so it was difficult for Hope to trust any older adult. But I waited for her to learn to trust me, and eventually she did.

One of the books I discussed with Hope was appropriately titled *We Weep for Ourselves and Our Children*. In the book, authors Joanne Feldmeth and Midge Finley discuss four building blocks in the development of a "healthy self": connectedness/community (family/friends), choices, virtue/value and sexuality/gender identity. Damage in any of these four areas, the authors contend, will stunt the development of a healthy self-image.[1]

Let's put it on a practical basis. If I were the mother of a little girl, I would want her to think in the following ways:

- I am loved.
- I have choices.
- I have value.
- I am a little girl who will someday be a woman.

But for Hope and other victims of sexual abuse, particularly those abused in childhood, it can seem impossible to feel a sense of belonging . . . a sense of being able to make choices . . . a sense of value . . . a sense of identity. In these areas, the necessary foundations of a healthy self-image have not been laid.

The confusion created in the mind of a child who is sexually abused by a family member or trusted friend begins a lifelong struggle in drawing appropriate boundaries. Also severely disabled is the ability to believe in anyone; the sense of

> *Sexual abuse attacks the "building blocks" of self-image*

connection/family is replaced by the inner warning, "Don't trust!" Instead of feeling, "I am loved," the victim lives with a sense of betrayal.

The threat of "Don't say no!" which often accompanies abuse, attacks the area of decision making. In the place of this important building block—the right to make decisions about one's own body—is a feeling of powerlessness. The victim thinks, "I have no choices." This feeling tends to become a victim mentality in adult life, a powerlessness and inability to make choices.

The building block of virtue is damaged by the warning, "Don't tell!" This command seeks to shift responsibility for the abuse onto the child. As a result she becomes overwhelmed with a sense of worthlessness and shame. The false sense of responsibility prompts the same questions over and over again, with no logical answer for the victim: "Why didn't I tell? Why didn't I try harder to get away?" If the victim does tell but is not believed, which happens frequently, the feeling is still, "I am bad."

It is easier to build walls than to feel all of this intense pain, so the victim says to herself, "Don't feel!" The sexually abused girl may lose her dreams of a wedding or a career. The abused woman has little or no hope for the future, knowing that no matter where she runs away, she will always carry her pain with her.

Dr. Dan Allender suggests that many victims of abuse may find themselves in one of the following three categories:

- A "tough girl," who builds a wall around herself so she won't be hurt again.
- A "good girl," who spends her life trying to make up for the past by pleasing everyone in the present.
- A "party girl," who gives away her body many times but never her heart.[2]

Allender notes that he has left men out of this description because he feels "less certain about the patterns that are characteristic of male abuse survivors." He does, however, make several suggestions regarding the typical relational styles of male victims of sexual abuse. Males may compensate for the damage by displaying physical or intellectual power, by becoming withdrawn and quietly hostile, or by compulsively talking about sex or acting out seduction.[3]

> *Without healing, victims of abuse often grow up to become abusers*

Without healing, those who are abused often grow up to become abusers. This fact should temper our abhorrence toward the abuser who is carrying the results of the "sins of the fathers."

God is a God of forgiveness, a God who takes the sins that we confess to Him as far away from us as the east is from the west. (Someone has said that the Bible says "east from west" because "north from south" is a measurable distance!)

Is Healing Really Possible?

A victim of abuse may ask: Can the wound ever be healed? Is it possible to recover? How and where do I find healing?

It's important to understand that sexual sin is like no other sin because of its effects—and aftereffects—on the body, soul and spirit (1 Corinthians 6:18), as well as its effects on others.

Paul states firmly, "Do not be deceived: Neither the sexually immoral . . . nor adulterers . . . will inherit the kingdom of God" (1 Corinthians 6:9-10).

Although the shame of guilt belongs to the abuser, often it is carried throughout a lifetime by the victim, who is doubly wronged: at the time the actual offense occurs and every time the memory is relived. The victim may live with her shame permanently, unable to recognize that she does not need to bear the responsibility for what happened.

The abuse victim feels dirty. Purity of body and purity of soul seem unattainable. She feels tainted, tossed aside and spoiled.

She is told that God is a God of holiness and righteousness. That simply heightens her sense of shame.

She is told that God is a God of love, of unconditional acceptance. "Oh, really?" she says to herself. "Maybe for normal girls, but not for me."

Shame is different from guilt. Guilt says, "I *made* a mistake." Shame says, "I *am* a mistake."

It's who I am, this shame
    not what I've done
    or where I've been
    but who I am.
Will I ever get beyond it?
Soar above it?
Put it behind me?
Will it always be a part of me?
Will it always be me?

It's who I am
  who I was
  who I will be. . . .
Shame makes me
  want to hide,
  want to withdraw.
It makes me feel inadequate
  feel ugly
  feel dirty
  feel spoiled
  feel ashamed of who I am.
Can anyone see past it
  through it
  around it?
Is there anyone who can know me
  know me completely
  and love me just the same?

Satan uses this sense of hopelessness to drive the victim of abuse into further sexual activity ("I'm not a virgin anyway, so I might as well give in to him"). Or she might want to find out if, given her background, she's "normal."

Cindy's Story

My (Joy's) relationship with Cindy began because her pastor told her she had to go for counseling. When she first walked into my office, she was not hostile. She simply did not want to be there. She did not want to talk to me, nor did she wish to relive memories of the past.

Over a year's time, as facts gradually emerged, I understood why. One afternoon we wept together as I finally discovered the traumatic facts of her childhood sexual abuse. We talked, prayed, talked more, prayed more. Cindy was able to draw pictures of the incidents she had been unable to describe verbally. Buried emotions came to the surface, and eventually almost unbearable memories began to lose some of their poignancy. Shame began to diminish as long-hidden secrets no longer provided the dark moldiness in which shame thrives.

But fears remained.

"Will I ever be able to respond normally to a guy?" Cindy brushed wisps of blond hair away from her eyes. "I don't even have the desire to hold hands."

We talked and prayed some more.

When Cindy left for college, her life changed dramatically. She amazed me with her leadership ability. When academics and unexpected physical problems challenged her, she persevered. Our meetings that summer overflowed with happy details of college experiences.

But a phone call several days after our last session revealed that there was an unresolved problem. "I really need to talk to you again. . . . Do you have any time? We . . . we could talk over the phone." But from the tone of her voice, I knew the conversation needed to take place face-to-face.

My intuition was correct, although I was totally unprepared for what Cindy had to tell me.

Since I knew Cindy had met a guy she really liked at college, I surmised from her phone call that she probably wanted to talk to me about her fear of physical closeness. But the counselor is not always right.

It took several hours for Cindy to reveal the secret she had kept all summer. She and her boyfriend, Ron, had engaged in premarital sex.

Just once.

"The morning after," Cindy said, "I felt like I had slapped God in the face." She called Ron, told him that she loved God more than she loved him and wanted God's will for her life more than anything else in the world.

Ron hadn't understood Cindy's feelings. To her great disappointment, he had shown no regret for what had happened. On the contrary, he had continued to pressure her for a sexual relationship.

Now Cindy was planning to go back to school and break up with Ron. At times she felt as though she almost hated him. Worst of all, she was again feeling the shame and worthlessness that we had discussed in the early days of counseling.

"None of us are good, Cindy." I looked straight into her eyes. "That's what the gift of God's grace is all about. If we were good in ourselves, we wouldn't need His grace. We have to go from thinking, 'I could never do something like that,' to 'There, but for the grace of God, go I.' "

I told Cindy how, during a terrible two-year period of my own life, I had struggled with accepting God's gift of grace. We talked about forgiveness—accepting God's forgiveness, forgiving yourself and picking up the pieces after doing something you thought you could never do. We also talked about failure—learning from your mistakes and going on from there.

Cindy went back to school and broke up with Ron. She also made the healthy decision not to date for a while.

At the end of the school year, when we met again, Cindy shared with me how meaningful Psalm 145:14 had become to her: "The LORD upholds all those who fall and lifts up all who are bowed down."

A Psalm of Promise

Psalm 139 became the "life Psalm" of another college student—Darla—who had painfully worked through an experience of sexual abuse. As we discussed the psalm, it took on new meaning for me as well.

I had labeled it as "the pro-life Psalm." It became precious to me when my doctor advised me, early in a problem pregnancy—our third son—that it was "too early to matter." He suggested a D&C rather than a pregnancy test.

As my friend Darla and I discussed the Psalm, I realized that it illuminates five concepts that are important to victims of sexual abuse:

1. God Knows Me.

> You are familiar with all my ways.
> Before a word is on my tongue
>   you know it completely, O LORD. . . .
> For you created my inmost being;
>   you knit me together in my
>   mother's womb. (139:3-4, 13)

2. God Has a Plan for Me.

God knows all about me, everything that has happened to me and promises to walk me through it. "All the days ordained for me were written in your book before one of them came to be. How precious to me are your thoughts, O God!" (16-17). God can make "all things"—even the trauma of sexual abuse—work together "for the good of those who love him" (Romans 8:28). Joseph said, after being sold into slavery by his brothers, "You intended to harm me, but God intended it for good" (Genesis 50:20). Darla saw this come true in her own life as she shared her testimony of healing.

3. God Understands My Feelings.

"If only you would slay the wicked, O God! . . . I have nothing but hatred for them" (Psalm 139:19, 22). God does not condemn feelings of anger toward my betrayer or abuser. However, God is my Avenger. When I take things into my own hands, I lose my place in line to see God's justice done. It's an awesome realization that God loves my abuser—not the sins, but the sinner—as He loves me.

4. God Will Help Me Analyze My Feelings.

"Search me, O God, and know my heart; test me and know my anxious thoughts. See if there is any offensive way in me" (23–24). We must "test the spirits" (1 John 4:1) and constantly be aware of Satan's subtle strategies. "In your anger do not sin"; continuing anger will "give the devil a foothold" (Ephesians 4:26-27). The familiar feelings of contempt (directed toward self and others) are not of God.

5. God Will Guide Me.

"Your hand will guide me. . . . Lead me in the way everlasting" (Psalm 139:10, 24). We are directed to "speak truthfully" in confrontation.

> Do not let any unwholesome talk come out of your mouths, but only what is helpful for building others up according to their needs, that it may benefit those who listen. And do not grieve the Holy Spirit of God . . ." (Ephesians 4:29-30).

Knowing that God will handle the eternal consequences means release from trying to do so myself and will result in peace.

The Power of God's Love

Think of the four factors in the development of a healthy self, mentioned earlier in this chapter:

- I am loved.
- I have choices.
- I have value.
- I am a little girl who will someday
  be a woman.

Is there an area in which you have problems receiving love, making decisions, feeling valued or accepting your womanhood?

God, who is Love incarnate, accepts you unconditionally. He desires to cleanse your life, to put your past as far away from you as the east is from the west. He promises to bury your sins at the depths of the sea. You can tell Him your past—all of it. You can trust Him.

Jesus understands your numbness and your fear of further pain because He too experienced abandonment by His Father, betrayal by His friends, humiliation by His enemies and agonizing physical pain on the cross. You are free to feel emotion and share it with Him.

The One who is holy reaches out to sanctify you. Rahab was once a harlot in Jericho; now she lives on in the "hall of faith" in Hebrews 11 because she believed. You too can have virtue and value.

Jesus waits to empower you. With His guidance, you can make decisions about your life and follow through on them.

Joy's Story

I (Joy) found that, over time, I could accept and deal with the fragments of my past—at least most of them. But some of the puzzle pieces didn't seem to fit into the familiar words of the "four spiritual laws": "God loves you and has a wonderful plan for your life."

I just couldn't understand what purpose God could have had in allowing me to experience sexual abuse when I was an innocent 10-year-old. (Since I was home-schooled, I had heard none of the "facts of life" that a child usually picks up in public school.)

It took a long time for me to comprehend that God's "Plan A" for my life may not have included sexual abuse but that God allows man to make choices—decisions that determine his destiny and affect the destinies of others. I came to accept what happened in my life as the result of irresponsible, sinful choices on the part of someone else: I was sinned against.

And now I had a choice—a decision as to how I would react to being sinned against. I chose to use my understanding of the emotions accompanying abuse—and the aftermath of it—to help others.

But my struggle wasn't over. God allowed my abuser to come back into my life. I thought that I had forgiven him, but I found myself experiencing floods of resentment and anger so strong that I actually felt physically nauseated in his presence. Anxiety and contempt surged through me each time I looked at him or heard his voice. Worse yet, vivid memories of the initial abuse—memories now almost 40 years old—replayed in vivid color on the screen of my mind. I had to take these steps:

1. I refused the feelings of failure, resulting from my seeming inability to cope, that Satan was throwing at me.

2. I recognized that I was reliving my childhood feelings of being unprotected and undefended and that I needed support and intercession from people who understood what I was experiencing.

3. I discerned the difference between the "old tapes" still re-playing in my mind (faulty or incomplete teachings from childhood, well-meant injunctions to "forgive and forget") and biblical truth.

4. I recognized that I was engaged in a spiritual battle and approached it as such.

5. I asked Jesus, who still wears His wounds so that He can always relate to us, to walk back with me through my painful memories.

During this extremely difficult time in my life, when I felt as if a surgeon's scalpel was playing with my emotional and spiritual innards, I learned some important facts about forgiveness.

Forgiveness and forgetting are not the same. The old question, "Can't you just forgive and forget?" is extremely hurtful to the victim.

My favorite way of explaining the forgiveness of God is that He chooses not to remember my sins against me. In the same way, as God enables me—and *only* as God enables me—I can choose not to remember another's sin against me. That does not mean, however, that I am capable of deleting all painful memories from my mental computer.

Forgiveness does not mean that I will automatically trust, respect or feel "warm fuzzies" toward the one(s) who caused me pain. It does not mean that I will naively allow him or her to reenter my world (or my children's world) without boundaries, guidelines and protective barriers.

> *Forgiveness is a decision and a continuing process*

Forgiveness does not mean whitewashing the wrong through excusing or psychoanalyzing the abuser. Forgetting minimizes the offense; forgiving does not.

Joseph was very straightforward about the way in which his brothers, the sons of Jacob, had abused him: "You intended to harm me, but God intended it for good to accomplish what is now being done, the saving of many lives" (Genesis 50:20).

Forgiveness does not mean that I take responsibility for what happened. I may have to let go of unrealistic expectations that the relationship will be healed or that the abuser will ever become a healthy person; true reconciliation requires honesty and integrity from two people, not just one. I simply accept responsibility for my attitudes from this point on. I do not "stay stuck" in the same place for the rest of my life.

Forgiveness begins with a decision, an act of the will, and is a continuing process. It involves allowing myself to remember the violations that were done to me and then asking God to take those memories, rather than clutching them to myself—hugging my hurts—as proof that the abuser does not deserve to be forgiven.

Forgiveness involves working through the hurt and anger that I feel at being violated, but not staying in an anger mode the rest of my life. It is also asking God to forgive me for my rage, my contempt and my hatred, and letting go of my desire for revenge.

Yes, forgiveness is a decision, a decision that I make to obey God rather than allowing myself to react sinfully to my abuser's sin. But it only becomes real to me as I remember the cross.

Many victims ask the question: Where was God when I was being abused?

The answer is this: God the Father was watching His Son, hanging on a cross.

Jesus Christ knew what it was like to be stripped naked, stared at, deserted and not believed by friends or family, even abandoned by God. His rights were taken. He suffered incredible physical and emotional pain, and the scars on His body still identify Him with all victims. He entered into our suffering so that we could be healed from the inside.

The story doesn't end there. On the cross, Jesus became the eternal Sacrifice, the Atonement for sin. His broken body became the bridge between sinful man and a holy God, and Satan's strategies to separate man from God were defeated. The One who understands the pain of the victim became the Victor!

Recovering from shame means that I learn to think and feel about myself victoriously, in the way God thinks and feels about me. The Bible clearly tells us how God feels!

[God] chose us in him before the creation of the world to be holy and blameless in his sight. In love he predestined us to be adopted . . . through Jesus Christ . . . to the praise of his glorious grace, which he has freely given us in the One he loves. In him we have redemption through his blood, the forgiveness of sins, in accordance with the riches of God's grace that he lavished on us with all wisdom and understanding. (Ephesians 1:4-8)

Someone has said that forgiveness means setting the prisoner free and realizing that the prisoner was yourself!

Think about It:

1. What past hurts have you experienced? What emotions or needs have those hurts created?

2. How is shame different from guilt? Think about this statement: "You are only as sick as your secrets and shame."

3. Do you see yourself fitting into one of Allender's categories: good girl? tough girl? party girl?

4. Do you *want* to be healed (read John 5:1-9)? Have you considered discussing your lifestyle with a trained Christian counselor?

Endnotes

1. Joanne Ross Feldmeth and Midge Wallace Finley, *We Weep for Ourselves and Our Children: A Christian Guide for Survivors of Childhood Sexual Abuse* (San Francisco: Harper, 1990), 10-11.
2. Dan Allender, *The Wounded Heart: Hope for Adult Victims of Childhood Sexual Abuse* (Colorado Springs, CO: Navpress, 1990), 158.
3. Ibid., 249-50.

Chapter 5

The Battle for Beliefs

Shirley called me (Joy) one morning, weeping inconsolably. A lonely, penny-pinching single mom, she had been befriended by neighbors in her trailer court. In turn, Shirley had attempted to nurture the relationship and had invited them to special events at her church. She had shared with them her testimony of release from the bondage of drugs and alcohol.

One afternoon the couple came for a visit, bringing with them some attractive clothes which, the wife said, Shirley could wear to church. After they had ordered pizza and sat down to watch a PG-rated movie, both husband and wife, individually, made physical passes at Shirley. Shirley resisted the passes and finally got the couple to leave, but she spent the rest of the night in sleeplessness, berating herself for having failed in the relationship and asking herself what she had done to bring on such an unexpected turn of events.

When she called her pastor and me the next morning, both of us told her the same thing: It was an attack of Satan, and she had won the battle. Since Shirley was, emotionally, still in recovery, we had a tough time convincing her that she was not a failure.

The name Satan means "accuser," and he lives up to the meaning of his name. That's why it is so important that we wear the belt of truth.

" 'What is truth?' Pilate asked" (John 18:38). Many of us ask the same thing. If we don't, we should. Satan would have us believe the lies of the world. We need to discern those lies, which sometimes come to us in sheep's clothing.

The Myth of Safe Sex

Sex between two unmarried adults can be "safe," the world says, if condoms are used faithfully. By "safe" they mean that there is no danger of being exposed to sexually transmitted diseases (STDs), including AIDS, or transferring disease to others. What the authorities fail to mention is that condoms rupture or slip off 7.9 percent of the time during intercourse or withdrawal.[1]

Twenty-five percent of women who become pregnant report that their partners used condoms.[2] "If condoms cannot always prevent pregnancy, which can only occur (normally) during one twenty-four-hour period of time each month," says obstetrician and gynecologist Joe S. McIlhaney Jr., "they certainly will not prevent STDs, which can be transmitted twenty-four hours a day, every day of the year. And germs are a lot smaller than sperm."[3]

When you climb into bed with someone today, you are also being exposed to all of that person's past partners and lovers. The germs are giddy with glee.

Every time you meet a potential date, you might feel tempted to use a checklist: "Hi, I'm Cindy. Do you have herpes? No? Okay, good. How about warts? No? Great. How about AIDS? Oh, really? And who else have you had sex with? Hmmm." Not a great way to respond after receiving a date invitation, is it? Besides, it's naive to believe that people who want you to view them in the best possible light would actually be completely truthful regarding relationships they themselves may want to forget.

It's also naive to believe that you won't get STDs or AIDS. A survey done by Burroughs Wellcome, a pharmaceutical company, found that "75 percent of Americans don't believe they could catch a sexually transmitted disease, even though doctors diagnose 12 million new cases, not counting AIDS, every year."[4]

People out there are getting STDs. It could be your neighbor, your coworker or your closest friend at church. Since STDs aren't on the list for appropriate mealtime conversation, these people may never tell you of their suffering. No one buys advertising space to tell others of their STDs although, come to think of it, that might not be a bad idea.

Consider these facts concerning the myth of safe sex:[5]

1. Herpes: 30 percent or more of single sexually active Americans have been infected and can pass this virus on to their partners. Herpes has no cure.

2. Human Papilloma Virus (HPV): This virus is carried by 30 to 46 percent of sexually active Americans. Now the number one reason women visit their gynecologists, HPV can cause venereal warts as well as cancer in both men's and women's reproductive organs.

3. Chlamydia: 30 to 40 percent of some groups of teenagers and college students have this STD. Doctors diagnose 4 million new cases each year. Symptoms are often absent or minor. Some experts consider this infection the most common STD in America. Chlamydia causes pelvic inflam-

matory disease (PID), which is the second most common cause of hospital admission for women of reproductive age (second only to childbirth). PID can cause sterility. The risk of infertility from chlamydia is almost double the risk of infertility from gonorrhea.

4. Gonorrhea: Roughly 168 out of every 100,000 Americans have this disease.[6] It may produce no noticeable symptoms but may cause PID and lead to sterility.

5. Syphilis: Approximately 32 out of every 100,000 Americans have various stages of syphilis, down somewhat from the peak in 1990.[7]

6. AIDS: Cases among women are increasing by about 17 percent each year. Of the 79,674 new AIDS cases among adults in 1994, 14,081 (almost 18 percent) were in women. Among those women, 38 percent reported contracting AIDS from a male partner.[8]

Is that enough to scare you?

Women often deceive themselves by thinking that they are not at risk because they haven't "gone all the way," but have stopped short of penetration.

Think again. All of these diseases are transmitted through body fluids. Syphilis can be transferred through kissing. Most nasty sexual disease germs only require warm, dark wetness. Herpes and venereal warts require only skin-to-skin contact.[9]

Women are at particular risk because of the nature of their sex organs. The costs of treating these diseases are

> *Total abstinence outside of marriage or a faithful marriage to an uninfected partner are the only sure ways to avoid STDs*

generally more expensive for women than for men. Infertility as a result of undetected or untreated STDs is more common for women than men. Many STDs have no symptoms. Those that are caused by a virus have no cure.

Authorities from the Centers for Disease Control and Prevention in Atlanta warn people to use condoms but fail to mention the 100 percent safety that sexual abstinence provides. When pressed, these authorities will reluctantly confess that abstinence is the only sure guarantee against unwanted pregnancy and STDs.

Joe S. McIlhaney Jr. relates the story of a group of sex educators who were asked by a lecturer, "If the person of your dreams, who you thought would be your best sexual match, were to approach you asking to have sex, but who also had AIDS, would you have sex with that person using only a condom for protection?" At first no one raised a hand. Finally, one person said yes. The lecturer then asked, "Why, if you are unwilling to trust condoms, are you encouraging students . . . to rely on them for protection against AIDS and many other diseases?"[10]

The Myth That Self-Control Is Impossible or Unwarranted

The world is willing to trust its health and life to the supposed impermeability of condoms, despite the lack of proper scientific studies ruling out the possibility of leakage of HIV,[11] because it has bought into the lie that control of the sex hormones is impossible or is an unnecessary restriction of rights or desires.

At a gathering of gynecologists, doctors warned their colleagues against overtreatment of HPV, despite the fact that several strains cause cancer. "There is really nothing we can do about [the spread of] HPV infection," Dr. Mitchell D. Greenburg of Graduate Hospital said. "Even condoms don't block transmission. . . . Don't upset a patient's sexuality over HPV."[12]

Psychotherapists have long preached the supremacy of feelings at the expense of responsibility. They may have confused repression with suppression. To repress desires means to deny that they exist. To suppress desires means to acknowledge their existence but to decide not to act on them.

There is nothing wrong with choosing not to act out your sexual desires. When the results of an act could prove harmful to any other human, including yourself, self-denial is honorable.

> *Self denial is an inherent part of the Christian life*

When an act would be contrary to the standards of God's Word, self-denial is godly. The moral fabric of our society has collapsed as a result of the failure to recognize the benefits of proper self-denial.

In *Restoring the Good Society*, Don E. Eberly traces the causes for the decline in America's values from "old-fashioned statesmanship," when people made choices based on the good of others, to today's rampant utilitarianism "of rights over responsibilities and of self-expression over self-sublimation."[13]

The victim status is too easily bestowed today. There are AIDS victims, welfare victims, crime victims, victims of poverty, victims of domestic violence, victims of broken homes, victims of media smear campaigns, victims of discrimination—on and on it goes.

People feel that they are not responsible for their faults and failures; they are just victims. Victimhood brings feelings of powerlessness. Feelings of powerlessness discourage any attempts to change.

The philosophies of Nietzsche, Marx and Freud have generated a mechanistic and material view of man. Their ideas implied that man is merely an animal who must blindly follow his instincts and that man must have the freedom of complete expression in speech, action and bodily functions. Their teachings have had far-reaching effects. While the power of political ideas is oversold, Eberly says, "the power of basic ideas and assumptions in the culture is rarely fully appreciated."[14]

> The 20th century has traded in moral man for economic and psychological man, subjecting him at every turn to either economic inducements or therapeutic treatments. If we are to recover as a society, the 21st century will have to recover a vision of man bearing inherent moral value and moral agency.[15]

We must see ourselves as God sees us: as unique, created, loved beings. We are not animals. We are capable of reasoning and weighing the possible consequences of our actions before we perform them. When we start with correct beliefs about the sanctity of human life, we can translate those beliefs into correct attitudes and proper actions. Only when we accept responsibility for our actions and their consequences will we be empowered to change.

The Myth That Sex Outside of Marriage Has No Consequences Beyond the Physical

If you have engaged in illicit sex and have managed to escape the scourge of pregnancy and STDs, then you're home free, right?

The world says that we can use our own bodies as well as other consenting persons' bodies in any way we like, as long as we take the proper precautions. The world has forgotten about guilt and the power of Satan.

The Presence of Guilt

Sexual sin is like no other sin. We wound ourselves to the very core of our being when we sin sexually. God created the sex act. As He designed it, it is a beautiful, intimate expression of knowledge, acceptance and love between a husband and wife. It is sacred. It was instituted before sin entered the world.

This divinely conceived act between a man and a woman is to be the crowning jewel in their relationship of mutual benefit and life-long commitment. As the bodies unite, so the spirits of the participants are to be enmeshed. "Therefore what God has joined together, let man not separate" (Matthew 19:6).

Each time you rise from the bed of a person to whom you are not married, you rend your spirit. Your inner self has a jagged, bleeding edge. The bleeding must be stopped.

Some persons run frantically from bed to bed seeking another heart to press against their bleeding one. Direct pressure of this sort produces an immediate feeling of restoration. But the original wound has never been sutured, and each additional encounter only leaves more tears, in turn causing more bleeding and necessitating more efforts at union.

In her autobiography, ballerina Gelsey Kirkland admitted to desperate striving for perfection in her body and her ballet. She never seemed to be able to separate her dancing from her love affairs. Despite having a succession of affairs with most of her male partners, she remained insecure, always hoping that her love with her next partner would be more romantic and fulfilling, yet worrying that the preceding experiences had ruined her sexually.[16] Gelsey had experienced the pain of breaking God's command and was lost in a search for meaning.

Other women who have wounded hearts as a result of sexual sins seek to cover the wounds with a thick layer of ce-

> *Guilt, loss of boundaries and lust are consequences of sexual sin*

ment. This denial stops the bleeding, but it also stops the heart from feeling. In numbing sexual drives and desires, the capacity for tenderness and compassion is also stunted.

In his book *Money, Sex and Power*, Richard Foster tells the story of a 78-year-old woman who was counseled by a friend of his. She had a myriad of fears and suffered from deep depression. During the counseling sessions, she was finally able to admit to a premarital affair when she was 16. She had not become pregnant, but she had carried the emotional wounds for over 60 years.[17]

Guilt is one of the strongest human emotions. Dr. James Dobson describes guilt as "an expression of conscience which is a product of our emotions. It is a feeling of disapproval which is conveyed to our rational mind."[18] Because these feelings and thoughts come from inside us, we can do nothing to escape them. Even if we turn up the radio, surround ourselves with people, immerse ourselves in work or flit continually from activity to activity, we can never escape the feelings.

Recognizing and examining those feelings are the first steps toward recovery. A wound can be healed through knowledge of God's forgiveness, together with time and distance, although scar tissue may remain as a reminder of the past.

The father of one of my (Deb's) high school friends was an alcoholic for years prior to his salvation. "God has forgiven my past," he said to me, "my family has forgiven me for the terrible way I treated them, and I have forgiven myself. But every single day of my life, whenever I look in the mirror to shave or comb what remains of my hair, I see the consequences of my sin." His face has a permanent reddish hue, the result of dozens of tiny capillaries that have burst. "God's not going to take those away."

The scars of sexual encounters outside the boundaries of marriage may not be visible to the naked eye. After Jacob wrestled with God, he forever walked with a limp. Even after your sin is forgiven, you may forever walk with an emotional limp.

The Loss of Boundaries

If a woman has tasted the pleasures of sex outside of marriage, then she must face the fact that continued temptation will exist. She has made sexual purity harder, though not impossible, for herself.

Someone has compared sex to sugar. The more you have, the more you want. If you always use three spoonfuls of sugar on your morning cereal and suddenly cut back to none, the first bowl will taste so disgusting that you'll want to feed it to your cat. But as you continue to eat cereal with no sugar, you'll gradually get used to it. Plain cereal will taste good, and three spoonfuls of sugar will make it sickeningly sweet.

Having advanced to a particular level of kissing or petting, it is tremendously difficult to regress to a lower level with the same partner. The human body was designed to prepare for intercourse, and that's exactly what it does.

It is also tough to set and maintain new boundaries in the next relationship. Let's say you have a new boyfriend, and this time you are determined to wait until marriage. But the lines of demarcation aren't there because of your past actions. Holding hands is not much of a thrill. Your mind fantasizes about the ultimate possibilities, weakening your self-control. You fall for the temptation to rush the early stages of physical expression, as in Kathy's experience. . . .

Kathy and her boyfriend ambled hand in hand along the snowy creek bank.

"I've wanted to kiss you so many times before, but I wanted our first kiss to be memorable." He paused, turned toward her and put his hands on her shoulders. "Tonight is perfect." He bent low and kissed her lips.

Kathy opened her mouth and explored his with her tongue. *Oh, no*, she suddenly thought, *I forgot. This is our first kiss. Why did I do that? I can't believe I did that. I'm just so used to it.*

She abruptly pulled away, ran a few paces through the snow, and stopped.

Her boyfriend stood stock-still. "Wow!" He shook his head. "Wow! Where did you learn that?"

Kathy just giggled. *I can't tell him the truth*, she thought. *He'd die if he knew what else I've done.*

The Lure of Lust—Present and Future

Since Satan knows he has been able to defeat you once in the sexual area, he will return with repeated attempts. He's found a weak spot which he will exploit to his advantage. He will try to lure you with his hook of lust—today.

You may find yourself inexplicably drawn to the people and places where you experienced that rush of passion. Your body may crave sex in such a way that you find it difficult to think

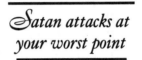

Satan attacks at your worst point

of little else. Tremendous amounts of self-discipline are needed to keep those heightened sexual desires in check.

Satan will also attempt to lure you with lust in the future. Sexual temptations are rampant in today's world for single and married persons. Marital fidelity can no longer be taken for granted. If sexual self-control is not learned during a dating relationship, it can remain a weak area during marriage.

Any person who has had multiple sexual partners, whether through previous marriage or not, can be tempted to compare technique. Such a person may become discontented with today's partner and fall prey to adultery.

If and when marriage does occur, the weed of discontent must not be allowed to grow, and this is the responsibility of the person with the past. Dave can't be asked or expected to caress the way Mike did because Dave is not Mike. Dave must be accepted and loved for who he is. To imagine being embraced by Mike when you are actually with Dave is lust—sin.

The Myth That Masturbation Doesn't Hurt Anyone

Masturbation has been an unending guilt trip for many Christians. The issue is rarely discussed, and when it is, speakers can seem overly judgmental or overly permissive. The Bible does not specifically mention it, but some basic principles can be applied to this issue.

One of the best treatments I (Joy) have seen was in a book I discovered during free time at a women's retreat. Some friends and I were browsing at a local Christian bookstore, and I saw the title, in bold letters: *Sex: It's Worth Waiting For!*

That evening, as we lounged in our hotel room, one of the women applied cosmetic masks to our faces which, she promised, would remove impurities from our skin. I complained to her that the women in my family inherit unsightly bags under our eyes, bags which elongate and broaden with age, and asked if the mask would do anything for that condition. She made no promises, but we settled back to await the arrival of facial purity and beauty.

As we did so, I leafed through my book, particularly noticing the chapter on masturbation. Years ago, the author said, people tried to scare others away from masturbation by telling them about bad things that would happen to them if they masturbated. The book included a list of some of those supposed results of masturbation. The last item on the list was this: "Dark circles will form around your eyes."[19]

My relatives and I must share a dubious heritage! I felt compelled to share the list with the group and we had a good laugh because, of course, none of the things on the list were true. And I feel compelled to share here some other quotes from the book, truths which are no laughing matter.

Masturbation is a self-centered act that neither fulfills nor satisfies. It is often practiced with the aid of sexual fantasy and becomes a dangerous foothold for the devil.

Author Greg Speck sees masturbation as sinful if any of the following patterns develop:

1. If the masturbation occurs in groups.

2. If the masturbation is done in conjunction with lusting (or fantasy) and/or pornographic material.

3. If the masturbation begins to control you, rather than your controlling it.

4. If the masturbation occurs after marriage, bringing a selfish focus into the relationship.

"People tell me," Speck adds, "that they masturbate to relieve sexual tension. The sad fact is that masturbation usually does not relieve sexual tension. You see, the more you masturbate, the more you want to masturbate. Often masturbation becomes an obsession."[20]

Speck goes on to outline steps to self-control, including praying specifically, noting your masturbation pattern and breaking it, filling your mind with positive things and being patient with yourself.[21]

The Myth That "It Could Never Happen to Me!"

This myth may appeal to a different group of people than the myths already discussed, but it is just as dangerous. God wants Christians to be "innocent as doves" but also "shrewd as snakes" (Matthew 10:16). This means that we cannot be naive or gullible. Regardless of our great spiritual knowledge, our position of leadership in the church or our feelings of superior self-discipline, Satan can and will attack when we least expect it. He may meet us on the mountain after an emotional high, or he may stalk us in the depths of an emotional valley. Being human means that we are vulnerable.

Faithe had been a Christian, her mother told her, since she had responded to an altar call at the age of four. By the time she was 12, Faithe stated, she had read the Bible from cover to cover. Faithe was the kid whose hand was always up in Sunday school, so much so that teachers had to tell her to give the other kids a chance. Faithe didn't find boys her age too interesting and the feeling was mutual.

Later, in college years, Faithe was also the young woman who was especially sensitive to the needs of a married professor, a seminary graduate who seemed so much more mature than her classmates. Not only was Faithe sensitive, she was vulnerable sexually as well. Although she thought it could never happen to her, she became involved in an affair.

A word of warning: If the person who "turns you on" spiritually is not totally controlled by God's Spirit, he may also turn you on sexually. The dividing lines between spirituality and sexuality can blur quite easily.

The research department of *Christianity Today* sent nearly 1,000 surveys to pastors regarding sexual temptation. One of the questions was: "Since you've been in local church ministry, have you ever done anything with someone (not your spouse) that you feel was sexually inappropriate?"

Twenty-three percent of those who returned the survey responded affirmatively. Sixty-one percent said that they fantasized about someone other than their spouse. Of this group, 39 percent said they thought that their fantasies were harmless.

In reference to this survey, Dr. Larry Crabb was quoted as saying, "I don't think those who consider sexual fantasies harmless really understand the deeper, compulsive nature of sexual sin."[22]

A corresponding thought related to this myth is, "I've learned my lesson; it'll never happen to me again." Remember the story of Samson, as well as this warning: "So, if you think you are standing firm, be careful that you don't fall!" (1 Corinthians 10:12).

The Myth That I'll Never Be Like My Parents

History has shown that family patterns are regularly repeated. The stronger the resentment and unresolved anger on the part of a child, the more focused she becomes on the problem and the greater the likelihood there is for imitation (although the recycling may not be evident to the person involved).

An example of this is when the adult child of an alcoholic becomes a "dry alcoholic." She may never drink a drop, but the family patterns of denial, silence, rigidity or isolation may be passed down practically intact. Promiscuity, in the form of physical actions or emotional fantasies, may also be part of the family inheritance.

The Myth That Sex Equals Love

In years past, men (who value sex) married women in order to gain access to sex, and women (who value security) gave their husbands sex in order to gain security;

> *If a man says he loves you and wants to have sex, don't assume that he really loves you. Sex does not equal love.*

both men and women learned love through the value of commitment. Today, although men still value sex and women still want security, many women give sex outside of marriage, hoping for security, and men gain nothing but an empty act. Neither love nor commitment is realized. In our culture, sex is called love and love is called sex.

What both men and women long for is relationship—intimate, knowing, caring, accepting relationship. We long for a relationship with our Creator and relationships with other humans. We long to have what Larry Crabb refers to as "Spirit Oneness, a turning to the Lord . . . to find security and significance, and Soul Oneness, a commitment to minister to the spouse's needs rather than manipulating to meet one's own needs."[23] Sex unites two bodies, but unless there is commitment and relationship along with the physical pleasure there can be no "Body Oneness."[24]

The sex idolized today offers physical oneness without true personal meaning. The sexual partner is a mere object for self-fulfillment.

The sex on television or in the movies is so idealized that it gives us a false sense of true love. It doesn't go on all night. Sometimes it's messy and awkward.

True love is getting up in the middle of the night to diaper, feed and console the baby you bore. True love is being patient when you are in bed (and trying to maintain your amorous feelings) while your spouse discusses business on the phone again. True love is planning, even writing on the calendar, a time to be alone with your mate. True love is interrupting the sex act to aid a child who is suddenly sick.

Love is commitment that lasts even when things get boring, dirty or hard. Love is willingness to minister to another person when you'd really rather do something else. Love is learning not to think of yourself.

Sex without commitment is the opposite of these things. It's demanding your own way. It's ignoring the lives of others, including the unborn. It's making yourself feel good regardless of the consequences for others.

Sex without commitment leaves the scene as soon as things get boring or hard or someone better comes along. It refuses to hear the pleas of others until it has satisfied itself. It thinks only of itself.

The Myth That Marriage Eliminates Loneliness

"I remember many Sunday afternoons," a divorced woman said, "when all my husband and sons wanted to do was watch TV or sleep through the day. I used to walk and walk through the woods for hours, feeling desperately lonely, and no one even noticed. In a way, it's a lot easier now. I still walk, but whenever and wherever I want to and I don't have to be back in time to fix dinner."

Even in good marriages, there are times of loneliness. Often there are protracted periods of time when one of the spouses is "away" or "out to lunch," either physically, mentally or emotionally. The resulting loneliness can be even more painful than the loneliness of singleness because the at-home spouse may feel abandoned, trapped or hopeless about the future of the marriage. Marriage carries no guarantee that someone will be there for you at all times.

Dr. Amos Meyers, who was my (Joy's) high school principal and early mentor and to whom I owe a debt I can never repay, lost his first wife to cancer. A subsequent friendship deepened into love and he married Jill Renich, a widow.

The Meyers' marital bliss was interrupted by two leg fractures and unexpected surgeries for Jill, who up to that point had always been healthy. Then friends and family noticed a change in Dr. Meyers that proved to be the beginning of Parkinson's disease. It was a time of clinical depression for this godly man and a time of loneliness

Happiness is not a matter of circumstances, but a state of mind

and terrible uncertainty for his wife. With children living at a distance (one was overseas in mission work), Jill had to place her trust only in God.

Thanks to the wonders of modern medicine and a great deal of intercessory prayer—and also to spousal faithfulness during extended hospitalization, temporary stays with in-laws and times of crushed hopes and dreams—Dr. Meyers regained his health and sense of humor. The next year Jill underwent chemotherapy and was hospitalized for extended periods of time.

Marriage does not eliminate loneliness!

The Myth That Circumstances Control Happiness

The young woman had come to a turning point in her life. Her past had seemed to die along with her young husband, and she could not go back to her childhood home or her childhood fantasies. And yet she knew that those voices from the past, those gods of her fathers, could pull her back into the old ways of thinking if she allowed herself to succumb to their influence.

She had to make a clean break with her past not only in her lifestyle, but in her thought patterns and her belief system.

Although she had no husband, no home, no money and no job, this young woman by the name of Ruth chose to look ahead. She knew that her most pressing need was not another husband. She needed to redefine her dream, to set new goals. In this agonizing time of recovery from grief, Ruth desperately needed a caring mentor to help her set those goals.

But she also knew that her deepest need was for a relationship with God, the true Source of security and fulfillment. Naomi, her mother-in-law, was the only person she knew who followed the path that led to God.

"Don't urge me to leave you or to turn back from you. Where you go I will go, and where you stay I will stay. Your people will be my people and your God, my God" (Ruth 1:16).

Ruth knew that the quality of her life did not consist in possessions or in the attainment of a husband. She was willing to remain unmarried in her pursuit of God.

Life in our sex-crazed culture demands wisdom to discern the truth from the vulture-like lies that ominously circle our minds. Sex outside of God's ordained boundaries can never be safe. Heavy consequences, which the world has desperately tried to ignore, diffuse or escape, result from misuse of God's gift of physical union with the opposite sex.

In looking for love we often find sex instead. When we find sex we often forget about our search for love not because we've found love, but because we've covered that God-given longing for relationship with sin.

Think about It:

1. Identify more lies of the world.

2. What lie do you most struggle with now?

3. Find and memorize Scripture to combat that lie.

4. Think of the physical areas that the "belt of truth" (Ephesians 6:14) covers. It was originally called the "girdle of truth" because it girded the loins (hips and lower abdomen) of a soldier. The loins were regarded as the center of procreative power. Why would an awareness of truth be important in this area of life? The expression "to gird up one's loins" meant to get ready to do something difficult or strenuous, especially in battle. How can we apply this

to spiritual warfare? How can you "gird up your loins" with the belt of truth on a daily basis?

5. Do you need to define or redefine a goal? Should happiness be a goal?

Endnotes

1. James Trussell, et. al., "Condom Slippage and Breakage Rates," *Family Planning Perspectives* 24, no. 1 (Jan.-Feb. 1992), 20.
2. Joe S. McIlhaney Jr., *Safe Sex* (Grand Rapids, MI: Baker, 1990), 38.
3. Ibid.
4. "Many in U.S. Naive about Sexually Transmitted Diseases," *Lancaster (Pennsylvania) Intelligencer Journal*, 14 February 1995.
5. Items one through three are taken from *Sexuality and Sexually Transmitted Diseases* by Joe S. McIlhaney Jr. (Grand Rapids, MI: Baker, 1990), 14-15. For more information on HPV, see also "Condoms Ineffective Against Human Papilloma Virus," *Sexual Health Update* 2, no. 2 (Medical Institute for Sexual Health, April 1994).
6. Centers for Disease Control and Prevention, *STD Surveillance 1994*, gonorrhea tables, 65.
7. Ibid., table 19, 73.
8. A.J. Hostetler, "AIDS Cases in Women Up Sharply," *Lancaster (Pennsylvania) Intelligencer Journal*, 10 February 1995.
9. McIlhaney, *Sexuality*, 20.
10. Ibid., 35.
11. Susan C. Weller, "A Meta-Analysis of Condom Effectiveness in Reducing Sexually Transmitted HIV," *Social Science Medicine* 36, no. 12, (1993), 1635.

12. Mitchel L. Zoller, "HPV Is Being 'Overdiagnosed, Overtreated,' " *Ob.Gyn. News*, 1 August 1993, 28.
13. Don E. Eberly, *Restoring the Good Society* (Grand Rapids, MI: Baker, 1994), 25.
14. Ibid., 34.
15. Don E. Eberly, "Even Newt Can't Save Us," *The Wall Street Journal*, 3 February 1995.
16. Gelsey Kirkland, *Dancing on My Grave* (Garden City, NY: Doubleday, 1986), 44, 135.
17. Richard J. Foster, *Money, Sex and Power: The Challenge of the Disciplined Life* (San Francisco: Harper and Row, 1985), 119.
18. Dr. James Dobson, *Emotions: Can You Trust Them?* (Ventura, CA: Regal Books Div., Gospel Light Publishers, 1980), 28.
19. Greg Speck, *SEX: It's Worth Waiting For* (Chicago, IL: Moody Press, 1989), 151-152.
20. Ibid., 148-149.
21. Ibid., 152-163.
22. "How Common is Pastoral Indiscretion?" *Leadership* 9, no. 1 (winter 1988), 3.
23. Lawrence J. Crabb Jr., *The Marriage Builder* (Grand Rapids, MI: Zondervan, 1982), 86.
24. Ibid., 87.

Chapter 6

The Battle to Control the Body: Combating Temptation

"Hi, Beautiful. Where've you been?" Tom pulled his white Cadillac convertible up beside Linda and put it in park. "You're looking better than ever."

"Thanks." Linda smiled.

"Why don't you ever come see me anymore?"

Memories of the warm brownness of his living room filled her mind—the antique mahogany desk, the rocker, the dark row of mahogany bookcases, the merino throw. She inhaled, unconsciously trying to get the scent of the room.

Lilac? She opened her eyes. The sight of a scraggly bush among the brambles by the road brought her back to the present.

"Because . . ." She shifted the weight of the books she carried. "I just don't."

Linda met his eyes. For several silent seconds she tried to transmit her inward resolve.

Tom shrugged. "Why don't you hop in? We'll take a ride to the country. I've been around here so long I forget what grass looks like."

Linda shook her head.

"Come on. It's just a ride. I'll bring you back. I promise."

Linda laughed. Tom knew such unique, quiet places. As she shifted her weight, her purse strap dropped from her shoulder to the crook of her elbow.

She sighed and said, "Just a ride, right. I bet you say that to all the girls."

"What girls?" He looked around in mock surprise. "There's nobody here but you and me."

"No, really, Tom. Thanks anyway. It sounds like fun, but I just can't."

"No? Well, maybe some other time." He put the car in drive.

"No, thanks," she said again.

Linda watched as he rounded the bend. The warm breeze caught a wisp of loose hair and tickled her neck. She shifted her books again. *There goes your life*, she thought. *You just said no to a great afternoon. And all you're left with now is* . . . she looked around . . . *nobody*.

Be Compassionate toward Others

A decadent chocolate mousse will be more of a temptation to some than others. For some, smoking or alcohol will beckon strongly, while others have no interest in them at all. Likewise, temptations to engage in sexual intercourse or foreplay outside the boundaries of marriage will cause some to stumble while others pass by unmoved.

Those who aren't tempted by sexual sin really cannot understand how difficult an area it is for those who are. This lack of understanding can easily lead to a harsh judgmental spirit which further alienates the already struggling person.

Within the Christian community, we seem to view those who have fallen into sexual sins as somehow more sinful than those who err in other ways, such as pride or selfishness.

Granted, sexual sin does bear consequences which last for a lifetime. Once original virginity is lost it can never be regained. The loss of self-respect, the loss of trust of another, the dissolution of a marriage, the breaking up of a family—these irreversible results can follow the misuse of God's gift of sexual intercourse. The aura of "extra-bad sinfulness" that often surrounds sexual sin (and leads to gossip) inhibits us from confessing our faults to others and seeking godly counsel. In God's eyes, though, the sexual sinner is no more unforgivable than the murderer or the liar.

Godly persons around us may never seem to struggle with the kinds of sexual temptations with which we struggle. We may feel that our minds are made up in terms of doctrine and beliefs but suddenly, out of nowhere, we find ourselves responding to strong, unexpected urges. We wonder if others have ever felt similar urges. We wonder if that unexpected urge is a sin.

Where does temptation end and sin begin?

Know Thyself

The point at which temptation ends and sin begins is subjective, an internal thing which only you can know about yourself. That knowledge comes as we grow in relationship with God our Father, learn to interact with the Holy Spirit and come to know ourselves and our areas of vulnerability.

"That's where honesty comes in," says Neal Clarke. "We develop that honesty by talking not only to God, but also with other people. We always need to remember that the person easiest to fool is ourselves."

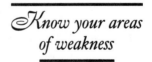

Know your areas of weakness

Jesus' temptation in the wilderness occurred immediately after a tremendous spiritual experience in His life: His baptism. The heavens had opened, the Holy Spirit in the form of a dove had descended on Him and a loving, familiar voice from heaven had reassured Him, "You are My beloved Son."

And then Jesus went into the wilderness, where He was without food for 40 days. By that time, He was probably very weak physically. Satan waited until Jesus was good and hungry—very vulnerable—before tempting Him to turn stones into bread.

But although Jesus was "tempted in every way," (Hebrews 4:15), He was on guard spiritually. Stanley Grenz points out that we are "on guard" when we ask ourselves: What are the everyday trials that repeatedly cause me to stumble? In what situations am I most likely to run into trouble?

> Matthew reports that in the wilderness Jesus was fasting and praying. Intimacy with His Father was fueled by times of spiritual renewal, and it played a key role in Jesus' ability to overcome temptation. . . .
>
> The ideal, then, is to live in the presence of God in such a way that everyday temptations go by unnoticed, not because we have unknowingly succumbed, but because we have unwittingly been victorious.[1]

Jack and Marsha, both new Christians, made a vow of engagement to each other and a vow of purity to God. They knew His power to renew their virginity, but they also knew themselves and their past experiences: Jack's barhopping; Marsha's first marriage, consequent desertion by an unfaithful husband and short-lived career as a belly dancer.

They knew that they could not expose themselves to the temptations that they would face if each of them lived alone during their one-year engagement (following their third date), so they chose to live with families within their church. Marsha lived with the pastor and his wife, along with some other singles, and Jack lived with another church family.

They knew—and their mentor, their pastor, knew—that they needed to postpone the discussion of sexual relations until the very last week of premarital counseling so as not to raise the level of sexual excitement. Marsha remembers that she wondered whether "everything was still going to work!"

"Everything worked great!" Marsha says, her eyes shining. "I still remember our honeymoon as the best vacation of my life. Please tell everyone that it was worth it to wait!"

Understand Male/Female Differences

Women rarely understand the instant turn-on a man feels when he sees a woman in provocative clothing or in various stages of undress, and in today's world that occurs continually.

Men don't realize the depth of disgust a woman feels when she learns that her physical relations with a man have been discussed and evaluated by a group of men and that she has been used—not as a person—but as a trophy in a case or a notch on a gun. Men are wary of the close friendships women have with other women and often remain suspicious even to the point of jealousy into marriage.

Both men and women misunderstand and underestimate how gullible some women can be.

Men's Instant Turn-On

One summer when I (Deb) was in junior high, my Sunday school teacher was in charge of cooking for a district men's retreat. She recruited me and some of my classmates as cooks and waitresses for the weekend. It was hot, the kitchen had no air conditioning and fashions of the late '60s included short shorts and tight knit tops.

As I placed bowls of scrambled eggs on a table, the man at the head beckoned to me. He slid his chair slightly away from the others and said, "I want to tell you something important about men, something you need to know and remember for the rest of your life. I've been watching you this morning. I watched you work last night, too, and I can tell that you want to do a good job. You want to do what's right. So, that's why I'm going to tell you this.

"I'm a pastor. I came to this retreat to focus on my relationship with God, but I'm having a hard time because I see you dressed in such short, tight clothing. You're a good-looking girl and I know you don't mean any harm, but you are causing me to sin.

"Do you realize that men are extremely attracted and stimulated by what they see? If you continue to dress like this, you are asking for trouble. Some man will take advantage of you sexually. It's very dangerous for a pretty girl like you to dress this way."

"But," I protested, "I don't have anything else to wear. I didn't bring anything different."

"I know," he said. "I'll make it through this conference. Just remember what I said whenever you go shopping or you're at home choosing what to wear."

The next morning I picked over the outfits in my suitcase and chose my longest pair of shorts—barely an inch longer than the pair I had worn Saturday. It wasn't much better, but it was the best I could do.

> *Understand that men may misunderstand your desires because of your style of dress*

This time the man gently touched my arm. "Thanks." He smiled. "I can tell you remembered what I said."

"This is my longest pair," I said. "It's all I have."

"Don't worry. I can tell you're trying. Thank you."

I know you've heard it all before, but it's true: Sight provides an instant sexual turn-on for men. Dressing modestly eliminates the subliminal messages that a more revealing fashion style may send. I've been married 15 years, and I'm still sometimes surprised by my husband's response or interpretation of a woman based on how she's dressed or not dressed.

Friendship Styles

Some men think nothing of discussing a woman's body or how far they have gotten with her sexually, mostly as a means of competitive jostling among other men. To a woman, each relationship is special, and intimate details of a man's body or of exactly what they have done together physically is rarely a conversation topic.

If women discuss their relationships with other women, it's generally for the purpose of seeking advice or perspective. It's what Dee Brestin calls " 'marriage work,' endeavoring to strengthen her friend's marriage by helping her to see the situation from his perspective, by 'framing' the husband in such a way as to 'enoble [sic] him,' or by diffusing her anger with humor."[2]

A man often misunderstands these encounters and suspects that his wife and her friend will constantly side against him. A godly woman-to-woman friendship can help rather than hinder a male/female relationship.

As a precursor to "marriage work," a woman will confide in her close girlfriend in order to try to gain a proper perspective of a man's actions or words. For example, is she reading him right? Depending on his intentions, this second opinion may help or harm the dating relationship. If he is interested in only using her as a sex tool, a woman's girlfriend may alert her to the danger. If a man has honorable intentions, a close girlfriend will discern that and therefore encourage the healthy relationship.

Men generally have few close friendships, and they don't communicate their feelings on the deep level that women do. Men are goal-oriented; they are out to get the job done and to excel. They tend to have friends to join them in their activities—a tennis partner, a golf foursome or hunting buddies. Even in these situations, competition remains a strong undercurrent, albeit friendly, as they

Understand that some men seek vulnerable women

strive to obtain the most service aces, the lowest score or the biggest buck.

Competition, then, is not surprising in the sexual arena; some men want to know who slept with the most women, who has the best-looking girlfriend or who got the closest to having intercourse with a woman who has a reputation for chastity. Sexual prowess becomes a game for some men. Sex is the opportunity to score, to puff up the self-esteem and to become a man in the sight of other men.

How should these gender differences be handled? The first job is to accept them, whether they are right or wrong. A one-woman campaign to change the world in this regard is doomed to fail.

Realize that your reputation for chastity (or lack of it) may very well be broadcast across the campus, the church or the district singles' retreat. Men you have never met before may know more about you sexually than you'd ever imagine.

Vulnerability

Women, generally speaking, are more easily deceived than men. "Adam was not the one deceived; it was the woman who was deceived" (1 Timothy 2:14). When a man pays any attention to us, we think that it's because he loves us and is attracted to our character. Now, we're not man-haters. We love our husbands. Joy has three sons. Deb has three brothers (and lived to tell about it!). But we have to be realistic—men are not always what they seem to be. Many of them will tell a woman anything in order to get her where they want her, and where they want her might be in bed.

Some men seem to have hidden antennae capable of detecting females who long for acceptance or belonging. These women may unknowingly send out signals of distress or vulnerability.

One interpretation of the end of the eighth chapter of Song of Solomon is that the wall mentioned in verse nine symbolizes chastity and the door its opposite. In his commentary, Charles John Ellicott says if a young girl grows to womanhood and remains a virgin, "inaccessible to seduction," she can be given away in marriage by her friends and family with full confidence.

If a young woman is a door, however, extra precautions will need to be taken to guard her honor and safeguard her virginity. Ellicott says, "This passage is one of the strongest arguments for the theory that chaste wedded love is the theme of this book. . . ."[3]

Are you easily deceived?

What is implied here is that some women are more vulnerable to loss of virginity than others. Praise to those Christian men who don't take advantage of a woman's desire for loving care. Would that more men took it upon themselves to safeguard a woman's sexuality regardless of whether or not she is an easy prey.

Joy recently dealt with a heartbreaking rape case. The woman had been molested by a particular male years before. She had moved away and, after a number of years, was back in the area with a husband and children.

When this particular male, accompanied by another male friend, knocked on her door under the pretense of welcoming her back to the community, she let them into the house. Wise? No. Gullible? Yes. Of course, the results were disastrous.

The significant men in this woman's life were not as understanding as would be hoped. They blamed her for her stupidity. It was perfectly obvious to them, because they understood the male mind, that this fellow was up to no good. But the woman was deceived. She, like her sister Eve, did not see the danger.

Women can see her point of view. She was probably thinking something like this: "Years have passed. He could have changed. There is a third party who could diffuse any danger. He might even be here to apologize. I'll let him in. I'll show that I've forgiven him."

The damage to this woman, and to her husband and their relationship, has been done. Empathy and compassion, not judgmental downgrading, toward women from Christian men would make the world a kinder place.

Godly suspicion and shrewdness toward men on the part of Christian women would help keep more women chaste.

Saturate Yourself with Scripture

To have victory over temptation, we must be discerning. To be discerning, we must know the difference between truth and lies. That can be very difficult unless we maintain balanced input in our lives.

A computer is only as good as the programming that controls it and the information that has been fed into it—a principle known as "garbage in, garbage out." Our minds are much the same. If we feed our minds on the Word, that's what will come out. If, however, we feed it garbage . . . you finish the sentence.

Someone has said, "What you feed grows; what you starve dies." What do you feed your mind?

We must know the voice of God. To know the voice of God requires saturation with Scripture.

Jesus, the Master of discernment, knew the voice of God. And on every occasion—whether in the wilderness resisting Satan, in the city rebuking the Pharisees or in the company of only the disciples—Jesus recognized the underlying threats and urgings of the devil.

Jesus knew Scripture so well that He could instantly spot its misuse by Satan. Jesus "saw through the diabolical scheme to get Him to short-circuit His calling to be the Suffering Servant."[4]

"To handle temptation," Grenz says, "we must grow in our awareness of God's own character, His ways and His goals. Jesus' example indicates, as well, that discernment means seeing through the falsehoods and rationalizations that could beguile us. . . . Being discerning means hearing warning bells whenever we find ourselves thinking, 'Everybody's doing it'; 'Just once won't hurt'; or 'I can do this and still be a good Christian.' "[5]

The Word must be more to us than just verses that we've memorized. We must read the Word, meditate on it, study it, breathe it in, pray it back to God . . . and live it. Remember that the sword of the Spirit—the Word of God—is our only offensive weapon in spiritual warfare!

Be Honest before God

Kris, a pastor's daughter, had an abundance of head knowledge, but as her singing career advanced she found it more and more difficult to protect her heart. She was traveling extensively, spending 14 to 18 weeks on the road, sometimes singing every night of the week at churches all over the country. "Do you know how many really good-looking men attend these churches?" she said. "Do you know how hard it is to stand up on a platform singing to

God, but noticing that cute guy in the third row?

"Let me tell you that was a real struggle! On the outside I was ministering to people about giving God control of all the areas of their lives, while I was struggling to keep a perspective on my purity and singleness. Anyone who is single knows that just carrying the stigma of being unmarried is tough; actually dealing with it is sheer torture at times.

> *"God knew my heart and knew my struggle"*

"I wasn't ready to accept the statement made by Paul so long ago, 'An unmarried woman is concerned with the Lord's affairs; her aim is to be devoted to the Lord in both body and spirit.' I was lonely and needed a human form to fill my void, didn't I?

"God knew my heart and knew my struggle and had a great plan in store for my weary, relationship-torn heart. You see, He had to break down my smart, intelligent, useless 'protection-from-impurity' lines to make me see that I had an area in my life that needed to be looked at truthfully. I needed to see that I was human, had needs and could do the right thing by pursuing the purity God had for my life."

Find a Mentor

Seek guidance from a mentor. The Bible

puts it this way: "As iron sharpens iron, so one man [or woman] sharpens another" (Proverbs 27:17).

Mentoring, in this context, is the process of helping a man or woman to achieve his or her maximum potential in Jesus Christ. Generally speaking, the mentor must have achieved superior rank on an organizational or professional ladder or must be an authority in his field as the result of disciplined work, study and experience. He or she should be interested in a protégé's growth and development and must be willing to commit time, prayer and emotional energy to the relationship.

"A mentor is not a person who can do the work better than his followers; he is a person who can get his followers to do the work better than he can," Fred Smith says.

It's important to realize that a mentor is not a "best buddy," an ever-ready counselor to be dumped on or someone who simply desires to be included in the family activities of the one being mentored.

Conversely, a mentor should not be ignored or dismissed when the protégé no longer finds the relationship useful, when the mentor is going through a difficult time or when mentor and protégé simply do not agree.

A good mentor shares the qualities that are required of pastors and deacons: He is willing to be a leader (1 Timothy 3:1); has mature Christian character and convictions (1 Timothy 3:2-3, 9; Titus 1:7-8); exhibits good management of home life (1 Timothy 3:4-5, 12; Titus 1:6); has been a believer for a relatively long time (1 Timothy 3:6); has a proven ministry (1 Timothy 3:10); has a good reputation with non-Christians (1 Timothy 3:7); has a sound understanding of and ability to use Scripture (Titus 1:9); and has recognizable spiritual gifts (1 Peter 4:10-11).

The Bible gives us examples of mentoring relationships: Moses with Joshua; Naomi with Ruth; Elijah with Elisha; Elizabeth with Mary; Barnabas with Paul; Paul with Timothy; Priscilla and Aquila, with Apollos.

Jesus was a Mentor who trusted, served, led and was vulnerable. Jesus mentored both genders; we need to be careful in that respect.

You may be asking: "But where can I find a mentor? My life is so ordinary; no great leader has shown interest in my life."

Here a Mentor, There a Mentor

At one time I (Joy) went to great lengths to sit at the feet of speakers and authors I respected. I remember a particular time when, at a public gathering, I followed a well-known woman to a restroom twice in an effort to speak with her alone. The first time she was polite; the second time she was a bit irritated. I was smart enough to back off.

When one of my favorite authors left her husband after writing a book about how great he was, I felt disillusioned. I began to see that God wanted me to "bloom where I was planted" instead of running all over the country taking notes on what famous people were saying. As I took care of my responsibilities, He supplied role models for me.

One of my mentors was a neighbor, Carole Reece, who modeled dedication to her husband and to his ministry, which often required him to spend long hours on the road away from her. (Today they have a ministry together in Jerusalem.) In my home church I watched women— some of whom had not completed high school—honor the Lord through ceaseless prayer, consistent Bible study and careful encouragement of younger women.

Another mentor was a sister-in-law, Ramona. She introduced me to Christian nonfiction, and my favorite author became an indirect mentor.

At a local print shop I met a certified marriage and family counselor, Ruth Dourte, who became my mentor, then my friend and then a co-author.

Years after I gave up on trailing famous people, my former high school principal introduced me to his second wife, Jill Renich-Meyers. Jill prayed for me, encouraged me to learn computer skills (she began at age 70) and took seminary classes with me. And she was a fellow writer. Much more important, she was my mentor and friend.

In recent years I've had many opportunities to return the favor. Once I was the one mentored; now, by God's grace, I can mentor others.

Why are men and women of today so afraid to become the mentors described in Titus 2—the listeners, teachers and encouragers who by lifestyles as well as words transmit holiness and wholeness? Graying hair does not need to be a liability; rather, it can be a mark of credibility!

A Mentor at Work

Kris (mentioned earlier) knew that she needed help and she wasn't afraid to admit her struggles to others. She sought, and God provided, mentors—women who played a strategic part in the development of her protection plan.

Her first mentor asked tough questions. She asked Kris what God was calling her to become and what she was willing to risk or sacrifice in order to obey.

"She went right for the jugular," Kris remembers, "with the next assignment: 'I want you to make a list of all the people in your life that you care about. List the qualities they possess that you feel enrich your life. Then write down the description of what you want your future mate to be like.' "

It was a long list, Kris said.

Kris's mentor showed her that God could be all of the things on her list and more. She quoted John 1:1, "In the beginning was the Word, and the Word was with God, and the Word was

God," and John 1:14, "The Word became flesh and made his dwelling among us."

"Kris," she said earnestly, "Jesus knew the flesh. He became Man so that He could empathize with our suffering. He truly is the One who understands you best because He has been where you are walking."

Jesus is the One who loved us enough to die for us. Jesus is the only One who ever fulfilled the true definition of love found in First Corinthians 13.

Almost every friend fails us at one time or another, and we fail our friends.

Look into the relationships in your life. See how they affect you. Then ask yourself: What needs are being met through these human relationships that God could not surpass?

Kris also formed a mentoring relationship with a single woman, a missionary who had struggled with the fact that God was to be her Husband, her Friend, her Confidant. This mentor spoke openly to Kris about her own struggles, being blunt about the lust and loneliness that had once consumed her.

Kris was amazed at the healthiness of the woman's current feelings and asked where the change had come from. Her mentor said that the Lord was making her a living sacrifice so that people could look at her life and see that even though she had struggles, God had given her the strength to place them on the altar every day. Sometimes she would have to place her feelings on the altar more than once, and sometimes they would writhe off of the altar as soon as she turned her back, but she could always return them to the altar.

"This is one of the toughest trials you will face," she told Kris. "I have to place my feelings on the altar every day, and you will be no different. If you find that it is lonely, my altar is only a step away, and you may use the side that is not worn down. Join me on my altar. We can walk through this together."

"How beautiful," Kris writes, "to know that I could share with her in the struggle for purity!"

Iron sharpens iron! Seek out mentoring relationships that will give you guidance, love and discipleship. Never be afraid to admit a weakness; we learn by being accountable to others. We are all people living out what God is making real in our lives.

Talk It Out

Did the dentist just lose his grip on the bib, or did he try to touch me on purpose? Is it my imagination, or is he leering at me? He is rather handsome. Does he find me attractive, or do I just want him to fall in love with me?

Ever been in this situation? It's hard to tell if the heart palpitations are a result of fear or erotic attraction.

Psychiatrist Peter Rutter urges women to talk about the issue when they perceive inappropriate sexual innuendos or advances coming from a doctor, lawyer, pastor or teacher. "If there is already a sexual undercurrent in the relationship, talking tends to defuse it by bringing the tension into both people's awareness. . . . [T]he very act of a woman bringing up boundary issues provides him an opportunity to relate to her reality instead of his fantasy world."[6]

Reacting to passions is easier than taking steps to stop the flow of emotions. In other words, allowing sexual arousal to control your actions comes more naturally than talking about perceived sexual actions. Yet talking is precisely what's needed.

Be aware, says Rutter, that when you do raise the issue, the man may use one of several defensive tactics:

- He may deny that he did anything sexual.
- He may put the blame on you and seek to make you feel guilty.
- He may reject you by ending the professional relationship.
- He may threaten to retaliate.[7]

In all cases, Rutter recommends that the woman leave the professional relationship.

In non-professional relationships where there is mutual attraction, talking about that attraction before beginning a love relationship can prevent hurts that might ultimately result from a relationship with no future.

"We were both feeling that there was something between us, more than just friendship," Sally said. "We thought, 'Hey, what is this?' So we got together to talk about our feelings, about if there was a future for us together. I've never been married. But he was still married to his wife, even though she had left him over 12 years ago. He felt it wasn't the Lord's will for him to file for a divorce. If she filed, fine, but he refused to initiate.

"So for now, we agreed not to date. I don't want someone with emotional baggage that they haven't dealt with, and there was no future for us right now. Starting a relationship would lead nowhere. I realize I may be single the rest of my life, but it's always better to obey God's commands. Always."

Watch Appearances

In Victorian England, the mere appearance of sexual impropriety was enough to incur condemnation. In George Eliot's *The Mill on the Floss*, the heroine leaves the village with a man to whom she is physically attracted. They spend one night on a boat, without physical union, and she realizes that she does not want to marry him. Even though she returns to her town, to her family and friends, she must now live the life of a social outcast. Her reputation is ruined. It doesn't matter that there was no physical contact between them; just the mere fact that there could have been—that the opportunity was there—is enough to prove her guilty.

Many singles today live apart from families, in their own apartments or houses. Such arrangements allow a myriad of opportunities for appearances of sexual impropriety. Inviting a male acquaintance into your apartment when you live alone is asking for trouble. And even if there's no spark of romance between you and you're just planning the next singles' retreat, your neighbors may assume that you have a physical relationship.

Try meeting instead at a public place. Or ask a married couple if you may use their house; just promise that you'll leave your white gloves at home and bring along your own munchies. I (Deb) would feel honored by such a request.

Another possibility is a godly roommate. Be honest with each other, and ask one another to be a visible third party whenever male guests are present.

Cut Off the Hand

One course of last resort is open to those in danger of committing an immoral act: amputation by our heavenly Surgeon. Matthew 5:30 says, "And if your right hand causes you to sin, cut it off and throw it away. It is better for you to lose one part of your body than for your whole body to go into hell."

Before you run for the knives, let's discover what this passage means. Verse 29 mentions the eye, which is the gate by which temptation enters. The hand, in verse 30, signifies the committing of the sin. The offensive sin, then, may be a struggle only in our mind or may involve another person. In either case, decisive action must be taken or we risk the consequences of our sin, causing collapse to the structure of our lives and possibly to our spiritual destiny.

We may know in our minds that decisive action is demanded, and yet we may feel powerless to effect those changes. We may earnestly desire to obey God, but we may find ourselves unable to exorcise the evil thoughts.

God stands ready to perform surgery. We must seek His scalpel. How do we do this? By asking Him to do anything necessary to remove us from the scene of the crime. By asking Him to do anything necessary to effect the needed result.

Don't ask these things lightly. You aren't asking God to change circumstances in another person's life; you're asking Him to change your life and to change you. Beware! God will answer, and there will be a cost. But blessings will ultimately result, and you will receive intangible deposits in your heavenly account.

Cheryl's handsome Christian boss often confided in her. How thrilling it was to have this respected attorney share his ambitions, fears and family problems with her. She felt that he must truly value her opinions. She was sorry that his wife didn't appreciate his good qualities, and she longed to be the bright spot of compassion and caring in his busy day.

Gifts of fine jewelry began to appear when he returned from business trips. They began looking for excuses to work late in the evenings or on Saturdays.

They began meeting at the park near her apartment to go jogging. Wouldn't it be so much more convenient for him, Cheryl argued with herself, if he could shower and change at her place instead of driving the whole way across town?

She splurged and bought fancy satin sheets and a matching bedspread so her bed would be ready if . . . She also bought a big box of perfumed soaps. As the smooth soap glided over her wet body, she imagined his hands caressing her . . .

Sometimes she'd awaken with a start in the middle of the night. "He's married, you idiot. He's got three kids. . . . I could be their—stop it! Don't think that." She mentally reprimanded herself. "How did you ever get yourself in this mess? You're a Christian. You know better. If you do this, you will ruin your reputation and his life."

With the morning sun came fresh resolve. But his smile and a mere whiff of his cologne brought back the desire.

She tried praying and becoming active in church. She even told her neighbor—one she didn't see too often that she was struggling. She lied, though, and said that there was no real man involved and that she was just fantasizing. So she came away feeling not better but worse. She thought about quitting her job; but then how would she pay the rent?

"Lord," Cheryl cried, "I want to obey. My flesh is weak. Don't let me commit this sin. Don't let me ruin these lives. Do something to change me. Take away my desire. I'm miserable. Do anything—whatever is necessary."

She threw away the perfumed soap. Shower time became cry-to-the-Lord time. Still she wanted him. She was consumed by thoughts of him.

Then she caught a cold. Two days later, when she woke up, her eyes wouldn't stop watering. Her morning coffee tasted strangely bitter. Peering intently at her face in the office restroom, she knew that something was definitely wrong with her face. One eye wouldn't blink or close. Her mouth sagged. Her smile was lopsided.

The doctor confirmed her fears; she had Bell's palsy. A virus had paralyzed the nerves of the left side of her face. Although there was no treatment, the condition was not serious, he said, but merely an inconvenience that would last from four to six weeks. "A small percentage of patients," the doctor added, "do not fully recover entire function of the nerves on the affected side."

The "mere inconvenience" put a clamp on Cheryl's former pleasures. The sun and wind tortured the eye that couldn't blink. She resorted to ointment that felt good but blurred her vision. Eating was agony. Liquids dribbled out at the side of the mouth that wouldn't close—and landed, unfelt and unknown, on her clothing.

Smiling was impossible. Laughing made her look like a drunken bag lady. Self-worth vanished with her good looks.

"God blessed me," Cheryl said, "with Bell's palsy. My desire for sexual experience was completely gone. I gained renewed repugnance for my sin. God gave me, along with gradual physical healing, spiritual healing and the strength to find a new job. Although it doesn't pay as well, I get by."

Think about It:

1. What temptations do you face? What Scriptures or Bible stories are pertinent to those temptations?

2. What is the "saturation level" of most Christians in terms of time spent watching TV, reading the paper, etc., versus studying God's Word? How might your life change if it were saturated with Scripture?

3. What is the importance of the sword of the Spirit in spiritual warfare?

4. If you struggle with sexual fantasy, what practical steps might you need to take? Jesus once asked a crippled man: "Do you want to get well?" Is that what *you* want? What is the cost of obedience regarding these steps? What is the possible cost of disobedience?

5. If nothing you do seems to help, have you considered the possibility of demonic oppression? Many Christians, even those involved in full-time ministry, have found that this kind of oppression has been present in their families for generations. (More information is available in, Mark Bubeck's *The Adversary and Overcoming the Adversary*, Ed Murphy's *Handbook of Spiritual Warfare* or "Seven Steps to Freedom" in Neil Anderson's *The Bondage Breaker*.)

Endnotes

1. Stanley J. Grenz, "Don't Take the Bait," *Discipleship Journal* 72, 1992, 41-43.
2. Dee Brestin, *And Then We Were Women* (Wheaton, IL: Victor Books, 1994), 15.
3. Charles John Ellicott, ed., *Ellicott's Commentary on the Whole Bible*, vol. 4 (Grand Rapids, MI: Zondervan, 1959), 402.
4. Grenz, 41-43.
5. Ibid.

6. Peter Rutter, M.D., *Sex in the Forbidden Zone: When Men in Power—Therapists, Doctors, Clergy, Teachers, and Others—Betray Women's Trust* (Los Angeles: Jeremy P. Tarcher, Inc., 1989), 169.

7. Ibid., 175.

Chapter 7

*T*he Battle to Control the Emotions: Managing Love Relationships

*L*oni and Cameron are looking forward to marriage in four months. Because the commute to Loni's job as a long-term substitute teacher requires that she rise weekdays at 5 a.m., she has little time to spend with Cameron, especially not late evenings. But after next week her position ends.

"I'm excited to be with Cameron more, but I'm worried too," Loni said. "We both want to save sex for marriage. Cameron lives alone in an apartment behind his parents' house. And it'll be a struggle to be self-controlled because I won't have to leave early to get my sleep. I'm worried about going too far physically."

The Necessity of Daily Decisions

Life consists of tiny steps along the path of our destiny. While some eight-year-olds know what professions interest them and can follow clear-cut educational strategies to meet their goals, some 40-year-olds find it difficult to choose even a hobby, let alone a job. The gifts of vision for the future and the self-discipline required to get there are not allotted equally to all persons. Some of us hardly know where we're going until we've arrived. We may hold a dim view of a desired goal, but we fail to perceive the steps or the sacrifices necessary to reach it.

I (Deb) remember my junior high Sunday school teacher saying that she first kissed her husband during their engagement. I thought that was the dumbest thing I'd ever heard. And that thought was the first step taken toward losing my virginity, although at the time I never would have believed that there was a connection.

You need to make a conscious choice to safeguard your sexual purity (as discussed in chapter 2). What remains, then, are the daily choices for sexual

> *Decide to maintain virginity, no matter how much you love your boyfriend and no matter how good physical contact feels*

purity within a love relationship. Now you must translate that decision into action while the person you care most deeply about may be urging you to do otherwise. This is a most difficult area.

Are we going to swim with or against culture's current? The path of least resistance always offers easier traveling and more companions, but the roar of the approaching falls may be drowned out by the party. Once we realize the danger of the falls, the sheer force of current and companions may make it impossible for us to swim to shore.

Some of us with good hearing are well upstream of the falls, but we're swimming in circles, unable or unwilling to expend much energy in continuous strokes. We stab at renewed sexual purity. We strike out with alacrity, only to be accosted by a friend floating downstream. To him, our efforts at fighting the current seem ludicrous. He's oblivious to the roar of the falls.

> *Save as much physical intimacy as possible for marriage. This includes being careful about showing affection early in the relationship*

Intending to save him, we call out. He responds by grabbing us and hauling us up on his raft. By the time we realize where we're heading, we've already gone miles downstream. We jump off of the raft and with renewed vigor swim a few strokes upstream, only to repeat the cycle again until one day we slide over the falls.

Sexual abstinence in today's society requires a conscious resolve plus a continuous effort to struggle against the tide of the world. This chapter is concerned with the seemingly small daily efforts at abstinence that, together, produce hard-core resolve.

After deciding to practice sexual abstinence, you need to take stock of your surroundings. Are you indeed on the path you've chosen? Examine the little steps you have taken recently within your love relationship. Are your words, actions, attitudes and thoughts obedient to Christ? What sexual boundaries have you established?

The Necessity of Self-Control

"I want to know," a 36-year-old sales assistant said, "how not to get in a bad position so that I go too far. What is too far?"

Over and over, respondents to our questionnaire asked, "How do I handle steps of physical and sexual intimacy in a relationship heading for marriage?"

You may be expecting to read something like this: Touching a member of the opposite sex above the waist with clothing on is okay. Touching below the waist is not okay. Touching without clothing is definitely taboo.

While strict, specific guidelines about physical contact before marriage can serve as alarm bells to ward off loss of virginity, they can also be used as tools to placate one's sense of guilt. *We want to experience as much of the joy of sex as possible without getting burned.*

Sinful nature is adept at finding ways to circumvent laws. Our ability, or inability, to handle the steps leading toward sexual intercourse is an area in which we may pride ourselves or berate ourselves. "If we claim to be without sin, we deceive ourselves and the truth is not in us" (1 John 1:8).

If we have a legalistic standard such as no lying down together or no removal of clothing, then we've given ourselves an out. We are tempted to think, "Maybe we went too far last night, but at least we didn't take off our clothing," or "I guess it's okay if I let Jim touch me that way; after all, it feels so good."

From this letter-of-the-law perspective, we could say that actual sexual intercourse is "too far" and that everything up to that point is "legal."

If you follow this route, and you do get married in the future, your honeymoon, instead of being one of excitement and surprise, will be anticlimactic and intensely disappointing. You'll think, "Is this all there is?" Your discovery will forever be a source of shame.

Of course, even for partners who are virgins, the wedding night can be anticlimactic. It takes time and patience for spouses to feel comfortable physically. In addition, even if you are a virgin, a steady diet of trashy romance novels before your marriage is guaranteed to make your honeymoon seem drab.

Understand the Spirit of the Law

Time and again Jesus taught that He did not come to destroy the law but to expand His influence over us into the realm of our thoughts and attitudes. Murder is not committed only with a gun or a knife, but with thoughts of hatred. In the same way, adultery is not only the mere physical act but also the attitude of the mind. (See Matthew 5:21-30.)

By this standard of measure, the question becomes: How much can I save for marriage?

The mind is the most powerful and the most overlooked sex organ. Sexual fantasy is dangerous because it leads to intense desire. If my hand is resting on my lover's knee but in my mind it's on his crotch, then that's too far.

Only you and the Lord know your thoughts and how far is too far. Only you know how much you can handle. Don't depend on your boyfriend to apply the brakes. You make the choice and keep on making the choice for virginity or renewed virginity.

Many books on sexuality depict a triangle with levels of physical intimacy on one side and levels of commitment on the other. These graphics are idealistic for singles in that they suggest an even, gradual progression toward sexual intercourse that is not possible for the Christian who wants to be a virgin at marriage.

Most relationships advance by steps of varying heights. Commitment, in the true sense of the word, is essentially nonexistent until after the marriage vows have been said. An engaged couple has indicated only a willingness to become committed, that is, to be legally, spiritually and socially bound at some designated point in the future.

That presents a dilemma for Christians who are dating. On the one hand, their bodies are sliding silently and ever so gradually toward the pinnacle of coitus. On the other hand, they are leaping hurdles discovering each other's ideas, feelings, likes and dislikes, methods of communication and ways of dealing with disagreements with no smooth progression in commitment level. How can they handle the dilemma?

Verbalize Limits

During a relationship the setting and maintaining of sexual boundaries can be extremely difficult. As two people become more enmeshed socially and emotionally, their bodies cry out for more physical inti-

> *Verbalize your limits; don't wait for your boyfriend to read your mind*

macy. Acknowledging one's desires and mutually seeking to raise standards of acceptable physical contact will help.

A man may view a woman's wish to talk about the subject as flirting, so if you initiate the discussion, you must be sure not to be misunderstood. State plainly that you desire to save sexual union for marriage. Talk about the meaning of a kiss, of holding hands. This isn't a verbal come-on but rather is the rational acknowledgment of the need to control passions.

During the five years prior to their marriage, Elisabeth and Jim Elliot talked and wrote about their desire for one another, but they maintained the physical limitations that they had established early in their friendship. The closer they came to marriage, the more sensuous their words became. Their words were not translated into action, however, until their wedding night.

In *Honesty, Morality and Conscience*, Jerry White lists five levels of communication. The lowest is cliché, followed by exchange of facts, exchange of ideas, sharing of feelings and finally total communication, which "depends on intuitive understanding and empathy as well as words."[1]

In your current relationship, at what level are you communicating? If you are only exchanging facts and ideas, then you are not at the point where the physical expression of feelings should be introduced.

Saying "I love you" to one another is an exchange of feelings, but simply because those words have been used does not mean that you understand each other's feelings on a host of other issues. What kinds of things make each of you sad? What kinds of things cause each of you to feel anger? How do you feel when you see injustice?

A physical expression of feelings begun before a verbal exchange of emotions will leave a woman feeling used. The man will be relating to her as an object, not as a person who has feelings. If intercourse occurs, both partners will be guilty of using each other as a release valve for their own sexual desires.

It can be extremely difficult to talk about feelings toward sexual intercourse, even to one's spouse of many years, and so it's understandable that unmarried couples will find such a discussion a monumental undertaking. But to safeguard or renew one's virginity, talking must be done. It takes a self-controlled and courageous person to do so.

Be brave enough to tell your boyfriend to stop touching you in a way that leads you to feelings of desire. If necessary, walk away from him immediately. Call your mentor or a trusted friend. Visit your pastor. Verbalize your sexual struggles to the mature mentors in your life and ask for help.

Engaged couples usually allow themselves added physical liberties, and Christian leaders often sanction such actions. Not all engagements, however, end in marriage. Will those liberties cause guilt and shame if marriage does not occur? Even if it does, what will be saved for the wedding night?

A 1992 survey of 1,000 *Christianity Today* subscribers found that couples who did not engage in premarital sex and were faithful during marriage were more satisfied with their current sex life than those who were involved sexually before marriage.[2]

Even in the secular world, *Redbook* discovered that "two out of three women would rather be a virgin if married today."[3]

Natasha, divorced and recently remarried, agreed on the importance of talking: "The first time around I felt the emotions and went with them. I took the physical expressions too lightly. The second time it was much easier to be in control of my emotions. Sex is so hyped, like you do it all night long, like it's so wonderful. I'm not saying sex isn't great, but [the hype] is just not anchored to reality.

"When dating my present husband, we had decided early on to save sex for marriage. A kiss to me means so much more than it does to the world. Because of past hurts, I needed security and caring before I could share a kiss. Part of me craved affection, but I also knew that without sex in the relationship we could spend more time talking. Sex would have hurt commitment. This way we were free to build a friendship first."

Religion and ethics columnist Michael J. McManus lists the following steps of physical intimacy in his book *Insuring Marriage*:

1. Look
2. Touch
3. Lightly holding hands
4. Constantly holding hands
5. Light kiss
6. Strong kiss
7. French kiss
8. Fondling breasts
9. Fondling sexual organs
10. Sexual intercourse

He suggests that if a couple has advanced to number eight or higher, their physical relationship has gone too far to safely refrain from coitus outside of marriage.[4]

Limit Time Together

In addition to talking with your boyfriend about physical limits, another safeguard is to limit your time alone together.

> *Watching someone and assessing character is much easier in the company of others*

Too much time with no specific plans other

than to be together is like starting a fire in the house: Sooner or later it will burn out of control.

"The wise way to form an opinion about possible partners is to find out their reputation, watch how they act in company, how they dress and talk and note whom they select as friends."[5] Watching someone and assessing character is much easier in the company of others.

"One thing that really helped us," Natasha said of her dating relationship with her husband, "is that we didn't spend a lot of time together. We wrote or called each other. That way we could talk. Once you get physical you stop talking."

Try writing letters, phoning each other or meeting in public where you are around other people. Have specific activities planned with set times to leave.

Flee When Necessary

Even when we take precautions, even when we truly love someone, sometimes flight becomes necessary. This flight may be in the form of the daily resisting of temptation, or it may be in the form of severing a relationship.

Marie and Harry successfully refrained from sexual intercourse until their marriage. They were successful because they had a plan and they made their plan work. While dating, Marie and Harry sat in the car talking only on the street where Marie lived, and at least once they felt it necessary to get out of the car and come into the pastor's home (where Marie lived) as a way of "escape."

Kelly faced a much different situation. She fell in love with a married man who said he was a Christian. She gave birth to his child. He begged her to marry him. He offered to leave his wife and start over with Kelly.

"In God's eyes," he told her, "we're married. I haven't had sex with my wife for as long as I've known you."

Kelly's response? She fled to the opposite end of the country.

"I had to get out of there," Kelly said. "Two wrongs don't make a right. It was wrong for us to be together, and even though I'm not wild about raising a child on my own, I know it's the right thing to do.

"If I had stayed he would have talked me into living with him. I love him, but it's wrong. So I quit my job, put my furniture in storage and came up here to live with my mom.

"I told him he's got to get straightened out with God and try to fix his marriage. It's no picnic, let me tell you. This is the worst time in my life, but my brother tells me that God will bless me—that my character is being developed. Well, if hardship develops character then I must have the best personality in this whole city."

The fact that we've sinned by having sex with someone doesn't mean that we are married before God or before men. Marriage is both a legal contract and a spiritual covenant. Sex outside of marriage is neither.

A quick marriage following sexual intercourse is a method some use to assuage their guilt. Such a marriage may cover up the consequence of pregnancy in the eyes of those who aren't good at math, but it doesn't atone for sin.

The Necessity of Balance

Maturity consists of finding the mean between extremes. Life's constant tensions pull us in one direction or another. For instance: How can a couple balance physical affection with self-control? How does one properly balance love of others with love of self?

> *Men seek a balance between emotional smothering and abandonment*

Both men and women need to find balance, but in different areas. Men must balance their desire for control with their need for relationship. Women must balance their desire for relationship with their need to depend on God alone.

Until I started the research for this book, I (Deb) always thought that single men were afraid of commitment. Mark Baker feels that "the issue is not a fear of commitment but a fear of abandonment."[6] Men commit to their jobs and to participating in sports games, he points out, but they find it difficult to commit to someone or something that can abandon them.

Men like to be in control of their lives. They also fear engulfment or being emotionally smothered, Baker says. So these two extremes—fear of abandonment and fear of engulfment—must be balanced.[7]

This balancing act takes effort. A relationship is a risk. A man may want a wife and long for emotional closeness, but at the same time he may be paralyzed by fears of potential hurt. He feels that he can only trust the most upright of women. How much easier it seems to depend only on oneself, as an emotional island, than to risk rejection. One of the greatest human fears is that after having divulged some previously hidden thought or feeling, one will be considered unacceptable for who one is.

Women long for the security of a relationship and may sacrifice everything, including their self-respect, to get it. Many women feel that they must be attached to a man at all costs. Emotional or physical abuse may even seem preferable to being alone. A woman in this situation may run from one bad relationship to another without pausing to contemplate her impulses.

True security is found in God alone, but sometimes He supplies that sense of security through a mentor or a support network. "In the multitude of counsellors there is safety" (Proverbs 11:14, KJV).

The Necessity of Good Character

So what is the single woman to do while she sits around waiting for men to pursue her? Knit?

Character development is the key. Men are initially attracted to physical beauty, but they maintain their interest in women who have depth of character. "The eye is the lamp of the body" (Matthew 6:22); a woman's love for the Lord will shine out unmistakably and, like the picture within the frame, be the attracting element.

When I (Deb) was an upperclassman in college, I had the opportunity to observe about 200 young men illustrating this point. The start of the fall term always brought a sense of anticipation as the males got their first looks at the incoming female freshmen.

One year the men practically quivered with excitement. Even some normally staid, level-headed guys got caught up in the action. The reason? A beautiful, blue-eyed, perfectly sculpted female freshman had arrived. The first time she entered the dining hall, all eyes turned toward her. Men stopped in mid-sentence to admire her beauty.

The girl sitting next to me sighed, "I can quit hoping for a date this year. They'll all be busy with her."

And they were. In pecking-order fashion, from the athletes to the politicians to the intellectuals, she was passed around. But in just two months, heads stopped turning when she walked into a room. She was no longer surrounded by admirers. In another two months she was occasionally seen eating alone.

A brave friend of mine finally asked one of the male students about the change. "Oh," he shrugged, "everyone found out that she's an airhead. I mean, there's nothing upstairs. All she talks about is how she looks. If her hair is messed up. If her fingernails are nice."

Men love a good chase and the sense of fulfillment at having captured a prize. Christian men generally value "sincerity, a good imagination, an interesting personality, a forgiving spirit, and a responsible attitude toward life."[8] Intellectually stimulating, non-self-centered conversation, plus the knowledge that a woman is physically unattainable to everyone, will pique the interest of a man.

> *Abandon your desires to God*

Naturally you can't expect all men to be waiting in line for you. The longest lines will always be outside the prostitutes' doors. Human nature gravitates toward what is easiest. But if it's marriage that you desire, one knock by a worthy, godly man is enough.

Godly character contains another element not commonly discussed today. Watch out. Here comes the terrible "M word"—meekness. Not mousy timidity or being a doormat for everyone to walk over, but Christlike meekness. Christ described Himself in Matthew 11:29 as gentle and humble, or in the words of the King James Version, meek and lowly. This same meek Jesus was the One who overturned the money changers' tables and chased them out of the temple with a whip.

Women need to develop the gentle and quiet spirit spoken of in First Peter 3:4. We like the Amplified Version of First Peter 3:3-4:

> Let not yours be the [merely] external adorning with [elaborate] interweaving *and* knotting of the hair, the wearing of jewelry, or changes of clothes;
>
> But let it be the inward adorning *and* beauty of the hidden person of the heart, with the incorruptible *and* unfading charm of a gentle and peaceful spirit, which (is not anxious or wrought up, but) is very precious in the sight of God.

Godly meekness allows you to recognize someone else as having ultimate authority over you. Jesus was meek; He learned obedience to His Father through death on the cross. "During the days of Jesus' life on earth, he offered up prayers and petitions with loud cries and tears to the one who could save him from death, and he was heard because of his reverent submission. Although he was a son, he learned obedience from what he suffered" (Hebrews 5:7-8).

What does meekness mean in marriage? A meek wife freely states her beliefs and opinions but sometimes needs to give the final decision (and responsibility for it) to her husband. A married man listens to and considers the wishes and thoughts of his wife, but he submits to God as his final authority.

Unmarried persons must give God the ultimate control of their lives. As both men and women practice seemingly small steps of obedience to God in every corner of their lives, their actions will result in beautiful characters.

A godly woman can reassure a man that his greatest fears won't be realized. In response to his fear of abandonment or hurt, she can admit her faults and sins and ask his forgiveness when necessary. In response to his fear of being smothered by love, she can demonstrate that she is ultimately trusting in God alone for her fulfillment and that she won't require him to meet her every need and desire.

The Story of Two Lives "Abandoned to God"

Trust in God and efforts at developing godly character can help us balance love of our treasures, whatever they may be, with love for God. God is a jealous God, and if we truly seek a relationship with Him, He will test us to see who or what is most precious to us.

"We are often hindered from giving up our treasures to the Lord out of fear for their safety," A.W. Tozer said. "This is especially true when those treasures are loved [ones]. . . . Everything is safe which we commit to Him, and nothing is really safe which is not so committed."[9]

My Utmost for His Highest and over 50 other books bearing the name of Oswald Chambers were actually written and published by Chambers' wife, "Biddy," who transcribed his messages after his death. She grew up in a family that could not afford to send her to school. Since her goal was to become secretary to the prime minister of England, Biddy practiced shorthand at home until she was able to transcribe at the rate of 250 words per minute. Despite her efforts, she did not attain to the position that she sought because God had other plans for her; He used her to minister to one of His "prime ministers."

But that did not happen early in life. Chambers was almost 35 when they married, and Biddy was 27. Their romance was preceded by an almost overwhelming time of what Chambers described as "four years of hell on earth."[10]

At God's bidding, he believed, Chambers had left London, interrupting a future in art, in which he was immensely talented, to teach in a Christian university in Scotland. Eight years earlier he had met and fallen in love with a woman named Chrissie, but while in Scotland he could only write to her and pray about the future.

In his prayer times during this period, he found himself wondering if he was holding something back from God. He wrote to Chrissie saying that he felt compelled to be alone with God. He felt commanded by God to cut all ties with her and wait.

"Shall I obey or disobey?" he asked.[11]

Chrissie knew that he was obeying God, but that didn't lessen the pain for either of them.

Chambers renounced his more recent dream of bringing the gospel to the world of art, and cut off his relationship with Chrissie. If he loved anything else more than God, he was ready to renounce it as well.

Years later, Chrissie said this about him:

> He was no "church window" saint, that is the last thing he would have desired to be—very real and human; not faultless, but blameless, a true knight of God, obedient to death, laying his "Isaac" unquestioningly on the altar. To such is given the Crown of Life.
>
> After this the seal of God came in floods of blessing, irrigating countless lives. "Because thou hast done this thing, . . . I will bless thee, . . . and in thy seed shall all the nations of the earth be blessed." God does not lead many thus, but He does lead some, and they must obey.[12]

Years later, Chambers met the woman whom God would use to preserve and perpetuate his messages.

The Necessity of Determination

Like Oswald and Biddy Chambers, we may not always understand the why or why not of a certain relationship or how things will work out for our good. But as we remain determined to obey God's commands and the leading of the Holy Spirit, we gain a deep sense of peace which can only be provided by God. This determination comes when our own feet are "fitted with the readiness that comes from the gospel of peace" (Ephesians 6:15).

When we wear God's shoes of peace, we don't get blisters. There is, however, no guarantee that the terrain on which we walk will be smooth, level and firm.

The Waiting Room

The future bridegroom had waited for a long time. But then, she was worth waiting for. He had known that years ago; he had known that she was the one the first time he caught a glimpse of those eyes, wide with wonder, watching a sunset. She was quiet, saying nothing, unlike her flippant friends, who glanced at the sky and then went back to discussing the boys they were watching.

Months earlier the buying ceremony, conducted by his parents and hers, had begun the betrothal period. He had gladly invested the large chunk of his life savings to ensure that she would wait for him. His bride would be as pure and untouched as she was when he had first seen her.

Often he dreamed of the day when he would be privileged to touch her, touch her so tenderly. But for now, obedient to custom, they were in a time of separation and preparation. He was carefully working on some fine furniture for their little home. She was preparing her wedding dress, the gown that would be as precious and pure as the bride herself.

Soon the night would come when he would go with his attendants to her home. She would hear the sound of the trumpet and come to the window. Her eyes would search for him, for him alone. Then at last he could claim her, could touch her, could escort her to the wedding feast. And when the feast finally ended, she would be his, his alone, for the rest of their lives.

Mary was pledged to be married to Joseph, but before they came together, she was found to be with child through the Holy Spirit. Because Joseph her husband was a righteous man and did not want to expose her to public disgrace, he had in mind to divorce her quietly.

But after he had considered this, an angel of the Lord appeared to him in a dream and said, "Joseph son of David, do not be afraid to take Mary home as your wife, because what is conceived in her is from the Holy Spirit. She will give birth to a son, and you are to give him the name Jesus, because he will save his people from their sins."

All this took place to fulfill what the Lord had said through the prophet: "The virgin will be with child and will give birth to a son, and they will call him Immanuel"—which means, "God with us."

When Joseph woke up, he did what the angel of the Lord had commanded him and took Mary home as his wife. But he had no union with her until she gave birth to a son. (Matthew 1:18-25)

What type of soles do your walking shoes have? Are they made of brave standards, godly character, sacrificial giving, persevering determination and unflinching trust? No clearly marked trail leads from the wide road of destruction over to the narrow road of life. The hike will be tough and may look impossible, but God will light the way and give peace . . . when you wear His shoes.

Think about It:

1. Review the comparison with rafting at the beginning of this chapter. Do you remem-

ber some situations in which you came perilously close to going over the falls? What have you learned from those experiences?

2. If you are currently in a relationship, are your physical actions pleasing to God? What specific sexual standards have you set with your partner?

3. Do you agree with the descriptions in this chapter of men's and women's fears and needs? Do you feel that men seek control more than women do? Are men more afraid of engulfment than women are? A friend recently described herself and the man she was seeing in this way: "He's co (codependent) and I'm indy (independent)!" She wanted a relationship, but she didn't know if she wanted to give up her hard-earned independence. How do you think attitudes have changed in the past 10 to 20 years?

4. What steps can you take to develop a more Christlike character? How can you put on the "shoes of peace" and be content with whatever is in God's plan for your life?

5. God truly wants to give us the desires of our heart, and yet sometimes it seems that He asks us to give up that which we love the most. Can you see how the desires of your heart have changed over the past 10 years?

Endnotes

1. Jerry White, *Honesty, Morality and Conscience* (Colorado Springs, CO: Navpress, 1979), 146-147.
2. "The Virginity Comeback," *SAM Journal* 12, no. 1, issue 108 (1995), 3.
3. Drew Reid Kerr, "Redbook Press Release," *SAM Journal*, 12, no. 1, issue 108 (1995).
4. Michael J. McManus, *Insuring Marriage: 25 Proven Ways to Prevent Divorce* (Nashville: LifeWay Press, 1994), 40.
5. J.I. Packer, *A Quest for Godliness: The Puritan Vision of the Christian Life* (Wheaton, IL: Crossway Books, 1990), 268.
6. Interview with Mark Baker, "Are Single Men Afraid of Commitment?", *SAM Journal* 11, no. 6, issue 104, 10.
7. Ibid.
8. Carolyn A. Koons and Michael J. Anthony, *Single Adult Passages: Uncharted Territories* (Grand Rapids, MI: Baker, 1991), 63.
9. A.W. Tozer, *The Pursuit of God* (Camp Hill, PA: Christian Publications, 1982), 28.
10. David McCasland, *Oswald Chambers: Abandoned to God* (Grand Rapids, MI: Discovery House Publishers and Oswald Chambers Publications Assoc., Ltd., 1993), 73.
11. Ibid., 75.
12. Ibid., 86.

Chapter 8

The Battle for the Future

Amy Carmichael once spent a day alone in a cave to contemplate God's will for her future. She brought her fear of the future to God: "Loneliness hovered like a spectre on the horizon."

She wondered whether she could endure years of being alone. The devil painted vivid horrors of loneliness—feelings of terror that she would easily recall 40 years later. How, she asked God, could she bear up under this burden?

God's answer to Amy was, "None of them that trust in Me shall be desolate."[1]

Peering into the fog of the future is scary. The mist swirls to form all sorts of monsters: loneliness, financial insecurity, selfishness and feelings of being abandoned by God.

How do we develop an intimate relationship with God that will enable us to withstand whatever looms in our future? From Jesus' model we learn the importance of prayer, not only as a spiritual discipline but also as an awareness of living each moment in the presence of God. Pray back the Word of God until it becomes a living part of you.

There are times when we lack strength and energy to wield the weapons necessary to combat temptation. Doubts close in on us, memories overwhelm us and our trust in God's promises is threatened.

> *Waiting on God for the unknown requires faith and trust*

In times like these we desperately need the shield of faith.

> But He said to me, My grace—My favor and loving-kindness and mercy—are enough for you, [that is, sufficient against any danger and to enable you to bear the trouble manfully]; for *My* strength *and* power are made perfect—fulfilled and completed *and show themselves most effective* in [your] weakness. Therefore, I will all the more gladly glory in my weaknesses *and* infirmities, that the strength *and* power of Christ, the Messiah, may rest—yes, may pitch a tent [over] and dwell—upon me! (2 Corinthians 12:9, Amplified)

The Necessity of Contemplation

What Are Your Options?

Every choice that we make *for* something contains an equal and opposite choice *against* something. Often this opposite is hidden. The world says, and we long to believe, that we can have it all. A decision not to have sexual intercourse with someone may mean the end of the relationship. A decision not to marry someone may mean being single for an extended time, even for the rest of one's life.

Conversely, a decision to marry someone who is not godly may mean a lifetime of regret. Even a decision to marry the most godly person one knows may mean a lifetime of self-sacrifice and self-denial. A marriage license does not come with a guarantee that we will live happily ever after.

And who of us can guarantee our own ability to meet the expectations of a spouse? One look into God's Word provides each of us with more than enough ammunition to blast our own sins, let alone those of a spouse.

Among all of this uncertainty, one sure promise is that God will meet all of our needs—not necessarily our wishes, but our needs. We may desperately seek a spouse to meet our needs, only to discover after marriage that those needs remain unmet.

We don't mean to imply that singleness is better than marriage or that childlesssness is more rewarding than motherhood. In fact, various studies show that married persons are healthier, live longer, and are happier than nonmarried persons. In an excellent analysis of the current myths of marriage, Dr. Moira Eastman of Australian Catholic University, says "both men and women benefit in terms of health, happiness, and life satisfaction from marriage. . . . In terms of health, men suffer even more than women from the lack of being in a marriage relationship."[2]

What we mean to stress here is neither marital state is *spiritually* inferior to the other. The truly inferior state is that of rebellion against, or mere complacency about, God's will for our lives.

Society is organized around expectations of marriage and childbearing rites of passage that signify adulthood. Feelings of sadness about not being chosen by someone for marriage or times of despair or regret about a broken marriage will come, but dwelling on those feelings is where trouble can begin.

Whatever side of the marriage or dating fence you're on, you can fall prey to the Cinderella syndrome that convinces you that "happiness was yesterday and will be someday but definitely is not now."[3] With such thinking, you're mistakenly trying to use external solutions to resolve internal dissatisfaction. Instead of accepting today's circumstances, the present is wasted by mourning for past relationships or marriages or hoping for the future ("Someday my prince will come").

What Are Your Fears?

So the biological clock is ticking toward alarm. Childbearing may be impossible if the "perfect spouse" doesn't show up by next year. What's a woman to do? Visit the sperm bank and raise a child who will not have the benefit of a father? Our self-centered culture increasingly finds this alternative acceptable. Christian women will face pressure to adopt this instant solution. But is there a viable alternative?

Look the fear full in the face. Lock yourself in your room and mourn the loss. The single woman past the age of childbearing has witnessed "the death of not one, but all her children."[4]

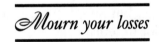

Mourn your losses

Although this is a major loss, the choice remains: What will you do? God is able to direct your maternal longings into a channel of ministry.

"All I ever wanted to be was a wife and a mother," Beth said. "I became a teacher because I wanted to be with children. But by age 32, with no marriage prospects, I was at peace with singlehood. I knew God would fulfill my desire somehow, although I couldn't imagine how. I hoped someday someone would come along, maybe a widower with children or a divorced man with a family.

"I had been in a relationship at age 27 that I thought was perfect and my family thought was perfect. When that ended short of marriage, I was devastated. I was forced to deal with the issue then. That was the turning point. I had to acknowledge God's control of my life.

"I feel so blessed now to be married and to mother an adopted child."

What Option Will Give Solid Peace?

In order to find peace, single persons—those divorced or widowed and those never married—need to seek God's guidance about marriage or remarriage.

The purpose of this chapter is not to examine the biblical grounds for divorce and remarriage, but simply to call for sexual abstinence prior to remarriage.

It is easy to get caught up in daily activities without taking time to contemplate where they are taking us. Reverend Tom Myers, who has developed a ministry of encouraging singles to seek marriage, says that many times young people become involved in their careers and activities without having determined whether they have the gift of singleness. Some great leaders of the Christian faith have had the gift of being single. But marriage is the norm. Many people today remain unmarried simply because of convenience.

The Christian life is strenuous. Paul compares a Christian to an athlete who beats his body or a soldier who submits to the rigors of the military (see 1 Corinthians 9:25-27 and 2 Timothy 2:3-5).

Finding a life mate is hard work. It takes dis-

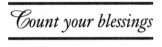

Count your blessings

cipline and determination to make godly choices. It takes continuous focus on scriptural priorities. Myers suggests that unmarried persons who do not have the gift of singleness need to take inventory and determine why they aren't married. The desire to make money or climb the corporate ladder, waiting for the "perfect" spouse, laziness or fear of getting hurt are not good reasons. According to Myers, men especially should begin the active pursuit of a godly wife.

Paul says that we are all to serve the Lord. The married person serves his family and in so doing serves the Lord. But the married person is busy working for the needs of the household, spending time with spouse and children. The single person, with no dependents, has more time to devote to other ministry areas. This is the blessing of being single.

A single aunt of my (Deb's) husband, now in her 60s, has singlehandedly organized yearly family reunions for as long as most of the family can remember. Knowing that she won't be able to continue forever, she is now training and encouraging the younger cousins to take turns planning the event.

My husband has fond memories of this aunt taking him and several other cousins on a trip to the beach, with no parents invited. "Aunt Ruth was always great fun," he says.

I (Joy) wonder if I would have survived the years of raising three sons, with a husband involved in an on-the-road evangelistic ministry, had I not had the consistent support of a single friend who loved to watch Little League baseball as much as I loved to read! Often Bev would take the boys for entire weekends to

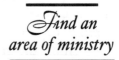

Find an area of ministry

visit her parents and to enjoy Knoebel's Grove, a nearby amusement park. Although there is no blood relationship, Bev has been and always will be considered a member of our family.

The Necessity of Giving

"Sure, it's Valentine's Day and I'd like to have someone give me flowers. Who wouldn't?" says 51-year-old Sharon. "But my life is full. I was a missionary for 10 years. I went to seminary. I work. I own a house. I'm involved with some singles here at church. I really have a ministry to them. I'm comfortable with what God has given me so far, but many of them are not."

One of life's paradoxes is the gift we give ourselves through sacrificial giving to others. Basic instinct urges us to grab the best for ourselves. Only as we learn to give with no thought of receiving something in return will we find the priceless fulfillment we seek.

Our God-created longing for relationship can be partially satisfied through giving to others—not by giving away our physical body, but by offering our acceptance, encouragement and support.

Single women can make lasting contributions in the lives of others by being involved in ministries of giving or serving. A good way to meet a mate is to be involved in a variety of Christian ministries. And even if you don't desire a spouse you can still be serving others and thus serving the Lord.

Use your gifts and talents for the Lord. One couple, for whom childbearing was impossible, spent 20 years of faithful ministry in the two- and three-year-olds' Sunday school class. Their love and kindness toward the children touched the lives of scores of parents.

You could be a leader for a teen missions trip. Not many married women have the flexibility to go to Chile for two weeks, and the cost of taking a whole family on such a jaunt can be prohibitive.

Consider spending a year or more on a foreign mission field. Many mission organizations welcome, and even earnestly seek, singles for short-term service.

Adopt a family. Offer to baby-sit so that the husband and wife can spend some time alone.

Be hospitable, not just to other singles, but to families as well.

Rebekah's Story

Another day. Another trip to the well.

The walk for water was as inevitable as the rising and the setting of the sun and less inspiring. But it was part of her responsibility as the daughter of the household—just a small part, but a very important one indeed, her mother always told her. Without water the household could not survive.

How many times had she traced these steps? Twice, sometimes three times, every day of her life, ever since she could remember.

As a child she had gone to the well with her mother. The well was an informal meeting place for the women of the village, a place to share small-town gossip. Sometimes strangers were there, fascinating strangers from exciting places, who for short moments of time were bonded with the villagers by their common need for water.

Perhaps her childish dreams centered around meeting a stranger at the well some day. Her mental picture was elusive; she could not assign a face to the tall, dignified form that entered her dreams by day and night. When she reached the age of 10, and then 12, and then 14, and when the village girls around her were becoming betrothed to the young men of the village, she tried to put away her childhood dream but it persisted.

Rebekah's busy mother did her best to replace her daughter's "dreamaholism" with a sound work ethic: "Always complete the task you've begun!" It seemed to Rebekah that she heard those words in her sleep, along with her mother's injunction to "always be kind to the stranger; someday you too may be a stranger in a foreign land."

Sometimes her father, Bethuel, would hear her mother's words and once again explain their meaning. He would reminisce about his Uncle Abram, who heard the voice of God speak to him, telling him to leave his country and his people and go to an unknown land to which God would direct him. Abram had believed that God would make him the father of a great nation—although, at the age of 75, Abram had still been childless.

God changed Uncle Abram's name to "Abraham," meaning "father of nations." Aunt Sarai's name, meaning "contentious one," was changed to "Sarah," meaning "princess."

Rebekah giggled at the thought. Her parents, too, still laughed when they thought about how Aunt Sarai had resisted the move.

"Why has your God not spoken to me, Abram?" she had argued. "Am I not the one who must carry this great nation in my now-shrunken womb? Am I to nurse a nation when I am 90 years of age? Why has your God not told me this great news?"

One day, like so many other days, Rebekah reached the well and began to draw water. She had performed this task so many times that her motions no longer required conscious thought or effort. She was totally unaware of her swift and graceful movements.

She did not notice the old man who stood nearby, watching her closely as she filled her large water jar and reached up to set it back on her shoulder. His request broke into her reverie: "Please give me a little water from your jar."

Her answer to the stranger was as automatic as her movements: "Drink, my lord," Rebekah said graciously, as she had been taught by her mother. "I'll draw water for your camels too, until they have finished drinking."

> So she quickly emptied her jar into the trough, ran back to the well to draw more water, and drew enough for all his camels. Without saying a word, the man watched her closely to learn whether or not the LORD had made his journey successful. (Genesis 24:20-21)

How many times did Rebekah run back to the well to draw enough water for 10 thirsty camels? She probably lost count. Being faithful to our responsibilities may involve looking sweaty instead of sexy!

Because of Rebekah's gracefulness and graciousness, because she was open to opportunity—even when it involved exertion on her part—and because of her faithfulness in completing her task, Rebekah was chosen to become a part of the promise that God had made to Abraham.

You may know the rest of the story. Rebekah did not see the face of her future husband until the end of the long, dusty, tiring trip. When they finally met, Isaac had just come from Beer Lahai Roi, "the well of the living One who sees me."

Rebekah's "wait as long as it takes and water the camels in the meantime" chastity enabled her to become part of the promise.

But, as with her Aunt Sarah, the waiting period may have seemed to go on forever. The trek through the desert on the smelly camels that she had so eagerly watered must have seemed interminable. And then her wait for a child . . .

As a matter of fact, she gave birth to twins—Jacob and Esau. But that's another story.

The Shield of Faith

How many years have you been waiting for God's promise to be fulfilled in your life?

Have you used your shield of faith to ward off the "flaming arrows of the evil one" (Ephesians 6:16)? "It'll never happen!" he tells you. "You misunderstood God's promise! It was just your own wishful thinking!"

I (Joy) was fascinated to discover that old-time shields were covered with leather and that the leather was soaked in water to actually extinguish the fiery darts—the flaming arrows—of the enemy.

These shields were not like the little plastic ones that we see today in the "armor of God" kits sold at Christian bookstores! Shields in biblical times were large and rectangular. Historical accounts tell us that they could be hooked together with the shields of other soldiers to provide a "moving wall" of defense.

That says something about the need for support in the heat of battle, doesn't it?

Deb K.'s Story

Deb K., a single friend of mine (Joy) who works at my alma mater, Messiah College, observes:

"Life in the Old Testament days seems so much easier than life in the 20th century. God seemed more audible and accessible at times. Right and wrong seemed more clear-cut. Choices seemed limited and less stressful. Basically, one's life seemed more simplistic and directed. Decisions still had to be made, but somehow it all worked out.

"One could look at Rebekah's life, at least the first part of it, and think this. Her daily routine of going to the well was typical for a woman her age. In her day and culture, watering a stranger's camels was no big deal; it was the hospitable thing to do.

"If God was at work through the prayers of others as well as her own, Rebekah probably had no idea of it. As the story unfolds, however, it becomes clear that God truly was at work and Rebekah was to leave her home and family to marry Isaac, a man she had never met. Yet, they loved each other almost immediately.

"I find myself thinking, *If only it were that easy in my life!* Rebekah was about 20 years old when she met and married Isaac. They didn't date or spend any time working on a relationship. Probably they just got married with the confidence that God had brought them together. I, on the other hand, am quickly approaching my

Choose to believe in God's sovereignty

mid-30s and am still single and chaste. I have dated and been in relationships. Yet, I still remain single and often wonder if God will ever bring me to my 'Isaac.'

"So how does someone like me relate to Rebekah? Well, I think it comes down to faith in God's sovereignty. Aside from age and cultural differences, I think we share the common denominator of trusting a sovereign and wise God. (Keep in mind that I'm referring to Rebekah's early years, before Jacob and Esau!) I guess you could say we share the philosophy of 'blooming where you're planted' and being faithful to your responsibilities.

"I'm sure Rebekah dreamed about that 'knight in shining armor' just as I often dream about that today. Yet she didn't allow that dream to keep her from the 'here and now.' After all, she had work to do and camels to water! And despite what might have seemed a lifetime of waiting to her, God's timing was perfect.

"I sometimes wonder why I am still single. After all, both my brother and sister have been married for over six years and have children. So what's wrong with me? Could I be that hard to love by another person? Am I not 'marriage material'?

"Sometimes I can't help making comparisons with family and friends. How can I not, considering my sister and I are identical twins? In many ways we look and act alike. So how is it she is married to a wonderful and loving husband and I'm still very single? As much as I've learned to accept and appreciate my individuality, I sometimes struggle with wanting to be more like my sister and have what she has—a husband and two adorable little boys. Even though my singleness has allowed me many opportunities to learn and grow, there is a part of me that desires to experience the life my sister and other happily married people have.

"I strive to be content in my circumstances, trusting God in every area of my life. Yet I'd be lying if I said it didn't hurt or frustrate me at times. Since I work on a college campus, I see many young relationships blooming. And when engagements are announced and wedding invitations mailed, sometimes I wonder, 'Why them and not me?' After all, they are so young and have plenty of time to get married. My time seems to be running out; statistically, my chances of marrying are quickly dwindling, and marrying another virgin seems almost impossible.

"At times like this I return to one of my favorite passages of Scripture:

> Trust in the LORD and do good;
>   dwell in the land and enjoy safe
>   pasture.
> Delight yourself in the LORD
>   and he will give you the desires
>   of your heart.
> Commit your way to the LORD;
>   trust in him and he will do this.
>
> Be still before the LORD and wait
>   patiently for him.
>   (Psalm 37:3-5, 7)

"I feel it's important to experience what God wants you to experience without holding back. God provided the opportunity for me to buy a townhouse at a good price and good interest rate. At first, part of me thought, 'I don't want to do anything that major on my own; I'll buy a house when I get married.' Yet the other part of me, the part that won out, said, 'Go for it, dwell in the land.' Since then I have been able to make my home available to family and friends (even to Joy, for a quiet haven to write and to work on this book)."

But godliness with contentment is great gain. (1 Timothy 6:6)

Believe God, no matter how impossible your situation.

Fred's Story

We cannot discard the shield of faith or we will find ourselves defenseless. We must believe that God knows what is best for us and trust in Him to lead us where He wants us to go.

Fred was 33 years old. A former Air Force officer, he was now president of a company. He thought he had "arrived."

"I was searching for what everyone else was searching for," he said, "whatever that was."

Fred was also a husband and a father. His family led the "country club life." But on July

30, 1964, while his wife was on a visit to Texas with their two children (a three-year-old girl and an eight-year-old boy), Fred received a message that his son was on the verge of death.

Fred got down on his knees and prayed. He found a Bible and began reading. Fred's son regained his health and the family flew home.

When he went to the airport to pick up his family, his wife took one look at him and said, "You've changed." As they drove home, she said, "I don't know what it is, but you've changed." Fred didn't know how to tell her that Jesus had saved him.

He kept reading his Bible. "Suddenly," he said, "there was a great gulf between me and my wife. One morning she said, 'I can't share this bedroom with you anymore.' Finally she said, 'I can't live with you anymore.' "

And so on the morning of August 21, 1964, his wife and daughter rode the train out of his life. His wife never returned, except for court hearings.

Fred kept reading his Bible. His son noticed a change in his dad and followed his dad's example in receiving Christ.

During the courtroom battles God convicted Fred of his hatred and bitterness toward his wife. God wanted Fred to love her, although he thought of her as his enemy.

He asked, "God, what do You want me to do?" The thought of any consideration for his wife, he said, was beyond him.

God said, "I want you to pray for her."

Fred asked, "What do You want me to pray for her for?"

"I want you to pray I'll save her."

He asked, "Lord, what do You want me to do? How long will it be?" (That's a reasonable question, Fred thought.)

God said, "I've waited for you for 33 years. What difference does it make?"

Fred began to understand that God valued her life and that he had to do the same. He said, "I don't know if I can do that. It is against every natural inclination of my heart."

But he prayed for her for six years. Then she remarried.

Fred said, "Lord, I can't believe it! I've waited all these years on her."

God said, "You've never waited on her. You've been waiting on Me."

And so, Fred says, "God and I went into this waiting hour."

His wife remarried again, and he said, "Oh, God, this is impossible. How can I keep loving her unless You fill me with Your love?"

She remarried a third time.

He got on his knees and asked, "Oh God, why is this happening?"

God said, "You're bitter."

Fred realized that he was, and he confessed his feelings to God. Then he asked, "Lord, what about her?"

God asked, "Lovest thou Me?"

Fred said, "But what about her?"

God asked, "Lovest thou Me?"

Fred said, "Yes, but what about her?"

And God asked, "Lovest thou Me?"

And Fred said, "Yes, Lord."

At the time of this writing, Fred and his wife have been divorced for 31 years. Fred has not remarried. He continues to pray for her salvation.

Fred says that before his salvation he was addicted to sex. On the night when he prayed to God in his family room, he was liberated from not only his sins but also the intense desire for sex. He knew immediately that he had been changed, although at the time he could not explain it. Today, Fred can testify that by the grace of God he has abstained from sex for 31 years!

"Young people should be challenged to give their sex organs to God," Fred says. "Do not commit a sin against the body; to do so could result, ultimately, in losing your soul."

We have related Fred's story, not for the purpose of condoning or condemning divorce or remarriage, but to emphasize that the biblical model of the prophet Hosea's faithful intercession for an adulterous wife still has meaning for us today.

Someone has said that faith is holding on when you want to let go and letting go when you want to hold on.

Believe that God has your good in mind no

matter how hard the situation is, no matter how terrifying the future looks, no matter how lonely you are and no matter how you feel. Praising God, even when you don't feel like doing so, enables you to hold onto the shield of faith because it reminds you of the character of God and protects the vulnerable areas of your life. Choose to believe in His sovereignty and live.

Think about It:

1. What is your greatest fear? Have you faced it head-on? Sometimes, when our worst fear is realized, we find that it's not so terrible after all. In Africa, groups of old lions, who can still roar despite the fact that their teeth have rotted and their strength is gone, terrorize hunters, who run away from the old lions and find themselves running into the young lions' ambush. "Running into the roar" may save a hunter's life.

2. What ministry could you undertake to help fill any sense of loss you may feel? How can you "dwell in the land"?

3. Reflect on the way in which shields were hooked together in battle in biblical times to form a "moving wall." Are you part of a moving wall? Have there been times when you needed to be part of one? What benefit could a moving wall provide to your community?

4. Have you experienced situations that, like Fred's, seemed impossible? Share with those around you some faith-building experiences of God's power in your life.

Endnotes

1. Elisabeth Elliot, *A Chance to Die: The Life and Legacy of Amy Carmichael* (Old Tappan, NJ: Revell, 1987), 79.
2. Moira Eastman, "Myths of Marriage and Family," in *Promises to Keep: Decline and Renewal of Marriage in America*, ed. David Popenoe, Joan Bethke Elshtain, and David Blankenhorn (Lanham, MD: Rowman and Littlefield, 1996).
3. Lee Ezell, *The Cinderalla Syndrome* (Eugene, OR: Harvest House, 1985), 44-45.
4. Margaret Clarkson, *So You're Single!* (Wheaton IL: Harold Shaw, 1978), 163.

Chapter 9

*P*rayer:
The Path
to Power

*P*lease, God, let them hear the doorbell, Maria prayed silently. *I know I never should have been out this late.*

Maria and her date stood outside the front door of the house where she'd recently rented a room.

"Are you sure you don't have the key?" Dave asked.

Maria shook her head. She pounded on the door.

"Well," Dave smiled, "why don't you just spend the night with me?"

"No, I can't do that." Maria's heart thumped so loudly that she had to put her hand over it to muffle the sound. She knew Dave's reputation. She never should have gone out with him in the first place.

Help me, God, she prayed.

She glanced at Dave. In the dim glow of the street light she could see that he was becoming angry.

"Come on," he commanded. "This way. There's got to be a window unlocked somewhere in this big house."

Thank You, Lord. What a good idea, Maria prayed. *Please let him find something*.

They stumbled around to the back of the house. Maria followed at Dave's elbow as they felt their way along.

"Here." Dave stopped. "What's this?"

"It's the sliding glass door."

"Hey, it's unlocked," Dave said. "There. This must be some sort of storage room or something. See ya."

"Yeah, thanks . . . oh, and thanks for the movie." She turned around, but he was already gone.

She fumbled her way into the hall and found a light switch. A tear slid down her cheek. She was safe. "Thank You, Lord," she whispered. "Thanks for taking care of me even though I did some stupid things tonight."

The Posture of Prayer

Prayer is preventive medicine as well as a healing remedy. It is better to ask for God's guidance first than to ask for His forgiveness later.

Spiritual warfare demands an offensive posture. We are commissioned to invade enemy territory and not just wait for the enemy to attack us. Our ultimate weapon is prayer—not as a last resort or a rear-echelon activity, but as frontline, offensive warfare which strikes a mortal blow at the enemy. In a sense, prayer is not simply a weapon we use; it is the battle.

We often hurry through times of praise in order to spend more time on our requests, but praise is one of the most powerful forms of prayer. Praise develops faith because it helps us focus on the character of God. Satan's attacks may continue, but faith forms a shield to repulse these attacks. It is always God's power that ultimately overcomes the enemy, but that power is often released in response to the obedience and faith of His people.

As we come to understand God's character and power, we can use "binding and loosing" prayer. There are times when we seem unable to sever unhealthy bonds. Attacks may hit personally and very unexpectedly, involving the most unlikely objects of sudden passion.

On a missions trip you may find yourself longing to be in the tanned arms of a fascinating tour guide or the attentive bus driver who's been watching you in his rearview mirror. Your mind tells you that they find gullible victims in every tour group, but your hormones aren't listening.

At times like this the image of Christ in Revelation 1:13-16 may help you to appropriate His "sharp double-edged sword":

> . . . among the lampstands was someone "like a son of man," dressed in a robe reaching down to his feet and with a golden sash around his chest. His head and hair were white like wool, as white as snow, and his eyes were like blazing fire. His feet were like bronze glowing in a furnace, and his voice was like the sound of rushing waters. In his right hand he held seven stars, and out of his mouth came a sharp double-edged sword. His face was like the sun shining in all its brilliance.

Ask yourself: Do I really want to stand before this powerful yet loving Son of Man, bonded into an unhealthy or unnatural relationship?

Sometimes the "binding and loosing" prayer needs to be prayed for someone else. Often, whether I (Joy) am in my car or in bed in the middle of the night, God will bring to my mind the name of someone who needs intercessory prayer. But it's important to remember that I can pray in the Spirit only as I am indwelled by the Spirit.

How much am I in control of myself? How much do demonic influences have access to my thinking processes, perhaps through lies I have believed for so long that I think of them as truth? How much do I allow the Word of God to saturate and purify my mind?

How much does God control each day of my life as I submit my will to Him on a daily, even hourly, basis? Perhaps I need to pray regularly, "Lord, I believe; help thou mine unbelief" (Mark 9:24, KJV).

The Power of Sexual Purity

The majority of this book has been written to encourage those struggling to balance their singleness with their sexual longings. We have based much of our writing on the belief that although sexual intercourse outside the God-ordained boundary of marriage is wrong, nevertheless, many have succumbed to the urgings of self and society to indulge outside those boundaries, not because God is not powerful, but because our flesh is weak.

But what of those who have kept themselves sexually pure? Will they be rewarded? Is all their self-control of any worth when the odds are likely that, if they do marry, they will marry a nonvirgin? Are there any dangers to sexual purity?

One hundred percent of the respondents to our questionnaire said that sexual purity would be worth it for a virgin even if he or she married a nonvirgin. Reasons expressed ranged from the self-respect of doing what is right in God's eyes, to having a gift to offer God and mate, to self-control that will be useful in other areas of life, to cutting down by 50 percent on potential difficulties with intimacy that the couple my face once married.

"Sexual purity," said a single bank teller, "is worth it because you do what is right in God's eyes."

"God asks us first of all to keep ourselves pure," a 33-year-old single man said. "This purity is a gift we can give to our spouse, as well as unconditional forgiveness and love if the spouse has not stayed pure. [If the nonvirginal partner] is repentant and a growing Christian, God can work because He can make all things new."

Clearly the singles we surveyed think other singles should abstain from sexual relations until marriage. The gift of an unencumbered sexual past is precious, something to guard as one would care for a priceless crystal vase.

Loneliness—the Path to Prayer

What of the sexual purity of those who never marry, who never experience the union of marriage? Can their longing for relationship be fulfilled? Yes, by all means. Marriage is never a prerequisite for healthy relationships on earth or with God.

John the Baptist, the apostle Paul and, most importantly, Jesus Christ were celibate and yet were fulfilled because of their relationships with God. All three had a strong sense of purpose for their lives—lives lived in service and obedience to God regardless of the personal cost involved.

The cost for John the Baptist included years of solitude in the desert followed by imprisonment and beheading. Paul's account of disaster after disaster in Second Corinthians 11:23-28 is a testimony to the cost of living the Christian life. Christ "was crucified in weakness, yet he lives by God's power. Likewise, we are weak in him, yet by God's power we will live with him to serve you" (2 Corinthians 13:4).

For singles the cost of obedience may include times of solitude and loneliness. You have a choice: What will you do with those times? Will you use them to deepen your relationship with God and as a springboard of service to others?

Contrary to what many people assume, loneliness is not caused by singleness. It is a result of humanness, of the Fall, of our separation from intimate communion with God. In the garden, Adam and Eve were naked in body and soul, transparent. Their relationships with God and each other were in perfect harmony until they disobeyed God's command. Suddenly they realized that they were alone. Terrified of that aloneness, they hid their bodies from each other and they hid from God.

Cain's distress upon being banished to a nomadic life was not because he would have to leave the land of his birth or be forced to struggle for survival or possibly killed. His plea was a cry of realization that banishment from God's presence meant he would not have the former peace that came through a relationship with God. "My punishment is more than I can bear. . . . I will be hidden from your presence; I will be a restless wanderer on the earth" (Genesis 4:13-14).

Since the fall of man, men and women everywhere have screamed in the pain of loneliness, terrified lest someone discover who they truly are, while at the same time longing desperately for the comfort and acceptance transparency brings.

Human relationships—no matter how deep, loving and secure—will never achieve more than weak stabs at the pre-Fall harmony. A relationship with God, however, is our means of sustenance, of gaining the blessing of transparency before God and others.

"Turn your loneliness into solitude," Elisabeth Elliot says, "and your solitude into prayer."[1] Bring to God your longings, your desires and your heartaches. Loneliness can be a gift from God to force us to the only answer for human pain: a deep relationship of dependence on our heavenly Father, the only One who always has our best interests at heart.

Jesus often sought times of solitude with His heavenly Father. Through the obedience of His relationship with God, He was able to bear the pain of death on the cross. Jesus freely offered up His life; no one took it. He laid it down of His own volition. Similarly, a virgin freely pours out her sexuality as a precious gift of obedience to God. Loneliness can be a wilderness that becomes a pathway to holiness, to God Himself.

Many people expend tremendous amounts of energy to maintain a facade of perfection. Even some believers tend to lie to themselves and to others about their sins. We know the things that we ought to say or do, and we know how we ought to feel; yet rather than acknowledge that we fall short of those goals, we lie and pretend to be spiritual. But once we relax in the knowledge of our significance to God, we can begin to relax around others.

Pitfalls of Purity

Ice skating was once my (Deb's) favorite hobby. On a whim last winter, I decided to retrieve my practically brand-new skates from the attic. Rummaging through a box of old window curtains and spare picture frames, I finally found them.

Although I hadn't used them in 15 years, they looked great. I smiled as I saw my maiden name in blue ink on the rubber guards, and as

I tugged to remove them, I was pleased to discover that they were not brittle. With my thumb and forefinger I tested the smooth coldness of the sharp blades.

Then I groaned. Between the edges of each shiny blade was a thick orange coating of that dastardly corroder: rust. From the side, each skate appeared perfect; only when the skate was turned upside down was the rust visible. I wouldn't be skating that day.

In today's culture a virgin may shrink from disclosing her sexual state. But within the confines of her heart, in those dark unused attic corners known only to God, there may lurk the rust of pride, silently corroding the usability of her life. A person who has saved herself physically must guard against this insidious force.

While the nonvirginal marriage partner struggles with the consequences mentioned in chapter 5, the virgin may be tempted to think that her efforts at maintaining sexual purity will set her apart for a higher seat in heaven. She may think that her purity has been guarded because of her superior self-control. She may believe that she is a better Christian than others.

Smug self-satisfaction leads to condemnation of others. Condemnation inhibits our ability to empathize with those around us and give them support and encouragement. The point at which we feel that we have much to offer others is precisely the point at which we fail to be used of God.

Works done for man's glory receive their rewards on earth, not in heaven. Sexual purity can become a form of earthly tangible success, not lauded by the world, but esteemed in the Christian culture.

God values communion with Him and a meek and contrite heart. The repentant fornicator has turned her heart toward God and received forgiveness from Him. The virgin needs to look with compassion, saying, "There but for the grace of God go I." Together they can join hands and walk through life as God leads. Together they can show by their lives the praise of God's forgiveness and His grace.

Living with Longings

The singles we surveyed listed a myriad of activities that help them deal with loneliness, but two keys stood out, each mentioned on half of the responses: prayer and friendships. Longings for relationship not filled by marriage can be filled through prayer to God as our heavenly Father and through friendships with those around us. We can bring to God our deepest and most secret inner longings and still remain sure of His love. To others we can bring those lessons that we have learned while on our knees in prayer.

Jane, a single woman in her 20s, was feeling confused and abandoned and desperately needed to discern God's will for her future. Following the advice of some out-of-state friends with whom she was staying, she rented a room for a month, furnished it with only a bed, bought a supply of food and prepared to "get alone with God." If she didn't receive an answer from God about what to do next, her only option was to go back home to live with her parents. Her relationship with her dad made her feel unwelcome there.

One morning as Jane was praying, she felt that God assured her that she would have a husband. She did not know when it would happen but she felt at peace.

Several hours later Jane heard a knock at the door and was surprised to find two married men whom she knew and trusted. They said that while they were driving through the neighborhood, God had brought her to mind and had given them a message for her: "Jane is not complete; part of her is missing." Jane gladly received this message as a confirmation of what she felt God had said to her earlier.

Twenty years later, Jane is still single. She says that she has not met a man she would want to marry. Did God lie to her? Did God lie to her friends? Did her friends lie to her?

We don't think so. But certainly our impressions of what we think God is saying to us often do change.

God assures you in Psalm 37:4 that He will give you the "desires of your heart." If we stop to think about it, we recognize that the desires of our heart change from our childhood through our teenage years into our 20s and 30s and later. So which desires does He promise to fulfill?

The promise of fulfilled desires is preceded by the admonition to "delight yourself in the LORD." If we truly sought to do that, wouldn't the desires of our heart change even more?

God also promises that "[t]hough the mountains be shaken and the hills be removed, yet my unfailing love for you will not be shaken nor my covenant of peace be removed" (Isaiah 54:10). And He says in verse 5 of that chapter, "For your Maker is your husband."

Could it be that God desires to be the all-sufficient One for those to whom He has given the gift of singleness? Has the culture, and even the church, accepted the myth that "normalcy means marriage"—resulting in many unhappy marriages in which people have settled for less than God's best?

Our friend Jane did not feel complete as a single, but does that mean that she would have become complete within a marriage?

Dr. Larry Crabb, a Christian psychologist, suggests that many people marry with the goal of completing each other. Instead of ministering to each other, however, they try to manipulate their spouses into fulfilling their own needs, which is not a realistic or fair expectation.

The State of Wholeness

Jane told about a singles conference she had attended and a visual illustration that taught her a valuable lesson. The speaker, Myles Munroe, placed half a glass of water and half a glass of punch on a table and said that the glasses represented a husband and wife, each incomplete. When the wife poured all of herself into the husband to make him complete, there was nothing left of her. When the husband poured himself into the wife to fulfill the desires of her heart, his glass was empty. As they kept pouring back and forth, liquid was spilled and the remaining mixture was diluted and not very tasty.

In order for a relationship to work, Munroe pointed out, both glasses need to be filled. If and when you go into a marriage, it should be in a state of wholeness; you need to know yourself, your talents, your abilities and your weaknesses.

Jane has been working toward her goal of completeness. She has moved back home, gets along well with her 80-year-old mother (her father has passed away) and is concerned for—not envious of—her sister, who is married to an abusive drug addict. Jane is the first person in her family to earn a master's degree. She is a supervisor at the department store where she works and she is seeing a Christian counselor, working through the hurts of the past, and continuing to send out résumés!

Sexual purity is a gift that we can give our future spouse, if and when we have one, and an offering of love we pour out to God. Our relationship with God as our Father and Husband gives us a firm foundation that enables a life of service to others. Perhaps, for the moment, we have crushed the forces that try to drag us into sexual sin; but we still need God to shine His flashlight of truth into all areas of our lives and root out any other sin patterns that may be there.

We must acknowledge our longing for relationships and submit the longings of our heart to the anvil of His love, to be forged into a precious offering of beauty to Him.

An Exemplary Case

Role models of chastity exist, showing us that purity (not perfection!) is still possible. One shining example was a vivacious, intelligent woman God brought into my (Joy's) life. I met Julie Fehr, a missionary, in the spring of 1994, four months before God unexpectedly took her home. A fast-spreading cancer interrupted Julie's plans to pursue a doctorate and the writing of a book during her year at Wheaton College as Missionary Scholar in Residence at the Billy Graham Center.

In 1964, young Julie said about being single, "I had worked very hard not to let that happen, but I didn't get a lot of cooperation in the right places!" She was sent to the jungle of Gabon, Africa.

This culture, Julie discovered, had a very different concept of who a single woman was, what she was like and how she should behave. The country of Gabon, given independence after colonialism, was now going through great upheaval. Old family values, clearly defined prior to colonialism, had been destroyed.

Within this context a woman did not have an identity of her own. She was first someone's daughter and then someone's wife or widow.

Early in her first term, Julie came face-to-face with this cultural difference when she was left alone overnight in a Tsogo village in order to practice the language:

> Julie tried to ignore the fear in her heart as she heard the sound of the four-wheel drive fade into the jungle. The chief and others came to welcome her to their village. Hospitality is very important among the Tsogo—they were going to take good care of this visiting "white child."
>
> The chief and his wife vacated their house so Julie would have a place to stay. Faces filled the doorway and windows as she began to unpack her belongings from their well-padded, dust-proof, insect-

proof and moisture-proof tin boxes. It was awkward—awkward for her and awkward for them.

As she slowly set up her table and camp stove and hung her mosquito net with many pairs of eyes following each move, she was aware of a conversation going on between the chief and a village elder. Since no Gabonese woman would be permitted to travel without her husband or children, Julie knew they were talking about her being alone and was pretty sure there was talk about her needing male company for the night.

She interrupted their conversation, assuring the men that, although it appeared she was alone, she really wasn't. God was with her. From the blank looks on their faces Julie knew she wasn't getting through.[2]

Then she saw the big double bed she was to sleep in and remembered hearing about certain kinds of village "hospitality." One village that happened to be on a truck route often provided overnight accommodations to truck drivers. "I had heard the missionaries talk about some of the problems they were having," Julie said later. "The young village women had venereal diseases because they were 'hostesses' to the truck drivers. It was part of the hospitality, part of the expectation.

But I didn't know that it applied the other way around, too."

Suddenly Julie realized that the villagers' sense of hospitality demanded that a sleeping partner be provided for her. With her limited command of the language, it was impossible to explain that she wanted to sleep alone. How could she make them understand? In a message she delivered shortly before her death, Julie described how God resolved this uncomfortable situation:

> A sudden inspiration hit me. Now is the time to unpack, show them what I brought, change the subject. I opened my boxes and unfolded my table. I then pulled out another package and took it into the bedroom, explaining, "That's my camp cot." . . . I was getting [the cot] set up, the doorway filled and the window filled, and people were watching. . . .
>
> Then suddenly the window got completely light, the room emptied and little feet went running through the village, shouting. They kept shouting the same words over and over again.
>
> They shouted it about five times before I caught what the words were: "It's a one-person bed! It's a one-person bed! She has her own one-person bed!" . . . Because of this camp cot they understood that I came to this village intending to sleep in a

"one-person bed." Who would have ever thought of it? Such a creative God, finding such a solution to the problem![3]

Perhaps the phrase "one-person bed" aptly expresses the physical or emotional solitude you have felt as a virgin or a renewed virgin in today's society. However, even if you sleep in a one-person bed, you don't need to live a one-person life. You can have a vibrant, spiritually healthy relationship with Jesus Christ.

Francis Scott Key, author of our national anthem, wrote a lesser-known hymn, "Lord, With Glowing Heart I'd Praise Thee," in which he states that we need to show our thanksgiving to our Savior with our whole life and not just our words.

> Let Thy love, my soul's chief treasure,
> Love's pure flame within me raise;
> And, since words can never measure,
> Let my life show forth Thy praise.

Sexually pure singles—and all forgiven sinners—can show forth God's praise by living their lives in humble and radiant obedience to God.

Julie Fehr explained:

> Wholeness does not happen because I'm married or widowed or divorced, re-

jected or esteemed by others—or not esteemed by others. That's not what makes me whole. Wholeness doesn't happen because I'm male or female, or because of my appearance.

Wholeness starts in the heart. . . . There is only one constant that will determine how you will respond to all the variables. It is your relationship with Jesus Christ.

Think about It:

1. How can you incorporate Romans 12:1 into your daily prayer time?

2. Do you feel the need to deal with habitual sin? The following prayer may be helpful:

Dear heavenly Father, You have told us to put on the Lord Jesus Christ and make no provision for the flesh in regard to its lusts (Romans 13:14). I acknowledge that I have given in to fleshly lusts which wage war against my soul (1 Peter 2:11). I thank You that in Christ my sins are forgiven, but I have transgressed Your holy law and given the enemy an opportunity to wage war in my members (Ephesians 4:27; James 4:1; 1 Peter 5:8). I come before Your presence to acknowledge these sins and to seek

Your cleansing (1 John 1:9), that I may be freed from the bondage of sin (Galatians 5:1). I now ask You to reveal to my mind the ways that I have transgressed Your moral law and grieved the Holy Spirit.

After you have confessed all known sin, pray:

I now confess those sins to You and claim, through the blood of the Lord Jesus Christ, my forgiveness and cleansing. I cancel all ground the evil spirits have gained through my wilful involvement in sin. I ask this in the wonderful name of my Lord and Savior Jesus Christ. Amen.[4]

Endnotes

1. Elisabeth Elliot, *Loneliness* (Nashville: Thomas Nelson, 1988), 127.
2. Lisa Rohrick, *Both Feet on God's Path* (Camp Hill, PA: Christian Publications, 1996), 48-49.
3. Message at Alliance Women's conference, Champaigne, IL, April 23, 1994.
4. Neil T. Anderson, *The Bondage Breaker* (Eugene, OR: Harvest House Publishers, 1990) 200-201.

Books by Joy Jacobs

They Were Women Like Me
(New Testament Women)

They Were Women, Too
(Old Testament Women)

When God Seems Far Away

With Ruth Dourte

One I Love

With Deborah Strubel

Single, Whole and Holy:
Christian Women and Sexuality